T0129578

The King's Princess

The true story of a little girl with
an astonishing gift given by God

SOPHIA CHANG

WESTBOW
P R E S S®
A DIVISION OF THOMAS NELSON
& ZONDERVAN

Cover illustrated by Eleah Ramos

This book is a work of non-fiction. Unless otherwise noted, the author and the publisher make no explicit guarantees as to the accuracy of the information contained in this book and in some cases, names of people and places have been altered to protect their privacy.

Scripture taken from the King James Version of the Bible.

Scripture taken from the Holy Bible, NEW INTERNATIONAL VERSION®. Copyright © 1973, 1978, 1984 by Biblica, Inc. All rights reserved worldwide. Used by permission. NEW INTERNATIONAL VERSION® and NIV® are registered trademarks of Biblica, Inc. Use of either trademark for the offering of goods or services requires the prior written consent of Biblica US, Inc.

WestBow Press books may be ordered through booksellers or by contacting:

WestBow Press
A Division of Thomas Nelson & Zondervan
1663 Liberty Drive
Bloomington, IN 47403
www.westbowpress.com
1 (866) 928-1240

Because of the dynamic nature of the Internet, any web addresses or links contained in this book may have changed since publication and may no longer be valid. The views expressed in this work are solely those of the author and do not necessarily reflect the views of the publisher, and the publisher hereby disclaims any responsibility for them.

Any people depicted in stock imagery provided by Thinkstock are models, and such images are being used for illustrative purposes only. Certain stock imagery © Thinkstock.

ISBN: 978-1-5127-1680-1 (sc)
ISBN: 978-1-5127-1681-8 (hc)
ISBN: 978-1-5127-1679-5 (e)

Library of Congress Control Number: 2015917383

Print information available on the last page.

WestBow Press rev. date: 11/21/2016

The King's Princess

Not to us, O Lord, not to us
    but to your name give glory,
      for the sake of your steadfast love and faithfulness!
- Psalm 115:1

Dear heavenly Father,

Anointing fire of the Holy Spirit, I invite you to please come inside my heart and fill the hearts of your faithful. I pray that you would bless every word, every sentence in this book. I pray that everything in this book is written in the name of Jesus Christ. This book is to bring glory and praise to your name. It is yours, Lord. I am simply a human being. I do not have the power, the wisdom nor the knowledge to write this book. I surrender myself to you, Lord. I am nothing without you heavenly Father. It is with the power of the anointed fire of the Holy Spirit that I have written this book. I ask that you bless every person that read this book and open the eyes of their heart, Lord so that they may see you and praise you. In Jesus name I pray, Amen!

A Christian
　　　is not someone
　　　who never goes wrong,
　　　but one who
　　　is enabled to repent
　　　and pick himself up
　　　and begin again,
　　　because the Christ – life
　　　is inside him.
　　　　　　　　　- C.S Lewis

Foreword

The message of God started appearing on a thirteen-years-old girl's hand and fore-arm at Frederick, MD. It began on the morning of December 14,2008. I happen to be a close witness among others and had the privilege of studying that happening.

Origin? Man-made (natural) or a Miracle (supernatural)?

In general, those writing would appear on her gradually in a process of a few minute, it will stay for about 5 to 15 minutes, sometimes shorter or longer, and then the writing will disappear gradually right before our eyes. It would repeat sometimes two or more times. If it is man-made, the skin would be easily infected and it may take a few days to get healed before you can scratch or prick another writing. Besides, there are various forms of writing as well. Like a scratch or prick mark, sometimes like an embroidery, or a raised letter on the skin. It is therefore concluded that it did not come from a natural (man-made) origin. It is truly supernatural/ a miracle.

Two Sources of Miracles

Two origins of super naturals are Demonic and Divine. There are approximately 800-900 writings appeared in the course of 5 years (2008-2012), about 85% to 90% are all scriptures and the rest are messages and pictorial forms, all related to the scriptures. The core messages of the writings are the coming of Jesus and about the end time. If the devil is busy with the Scriptures, what are the Bible believing Christians doing with their Books? And the devil would be the last one to tell us about the coming of Jesus and the end times. It is, hereby, concluded the origin of this miracle as Divine.

If it is Divine in Origin, why did God do it?

This miracle could be classified as "Signs and Wonders". Therefore, this must be something that should wonder us. It should not be something that we are acquainted with, or have experienced in our daily lives. Because, one of the purposes of Divine miracles is to draw attention of us (eg. Burning bush with Moses in the Wilderness) to Him so that He can convey His message to us.

All these writings were in line with the mind and the flow of the Bible and it all pointed to His Nature, His love to communicate with His beloved people, the end of time and His coming back which He eagerly prepared before the foundation of the world.

By: James Singzakhai

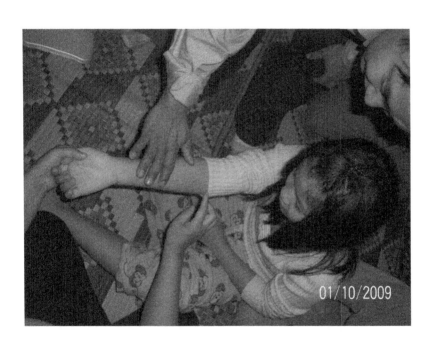

Sophia Arabella Chang

I was born in Myanmar and raised in Frederick, Maryland. I am eighteen years old, the youngest of four children. This is my first book.

I often have wondered, while staring at my laptop, how to share my testimony. How do I explain the spiritual gift the Lord had given me, the special message that my Heavenly Father shared with me? How do I explain the miracles that the Lord shown me? The truth is that even after 5 years of God sharing the message with me, I still don't have an answer for these questions. So with my faith in Him and with all the courage an eighteen-year-old can gather, I am writing this book that my Heavenly Father told me to write.

When God told me to write about my journey with Him five years ago, my first thought was, *Lord, how do you expect me to write a book when I can barley write my 2 page essay in school? Who would listen to 13 years old words?* I was worried and scared. Who would have listen to 13 years old words? We have waited 5 years for me to turn 18 years old to write this book. Even as 18 years old, I still had a hard time writing this book. I couldn't write a book; I don't know anything about writing. But the Lord said to trust Him. I realize that this isn't my book; this is His book - and with God, nothing is impossible. He has a plan for me, a plan to prosper and not to bring harm (*Jeremiah 29:11*).

Before you continue on reading, I do want to tell you that this book isn't your average book. This book is not inspirational or self-improvement book. Every word, every sentence was written with the blessing of God. This book is about a thirteen years old journey to finding what it really means to follow Jesus Christ (*Matthew 16:24*).

I was thirteen years old when I first came to *truly* know God. The reason I use the word "Truly" is because I was raised in a Christian home. I was raised between two religions. My father's side of the family is Catholic, and my mother's side is Pentecostal. My mother and paternal grandmother took turns bringing us children to their respective churches on Sunday. But as a young child, I didn't quite fully understand the words of God or who God is. To me, Sunday was just another Saturday, except we dress up and go into this big beautiful house for an hour. When I first came to know God, I didn't know who the Holy Spirit was or how spiritual gifts work. So when I was given supernatural gift, I was confused and scared. How does one fully understand such supernatural gift of writing from the Holy Spirit?

You may wonder what spiritual gift of writing that God has gifted me with. The biblical reference that may be the easiest to explain is the handwriting on the wall mentioned in *Daniel 5*, but instead of the wall, it is my flesh God uses as His wall. I'm sure you are having a hard time coming to term with this supernatural gift and is thinking, "what am I reading?" or probably regret picking up this book but this isn't a lie coming out of an 18 years old or a story that a 13 years old made up 5 years ago. You might have a hard time believing that God uses me in this way but the truth is the truth whether you believe it or not. A quote by **St. Augustine** says, *"The* **Truth** *is like a* **Lion**. *You don't have to defend it. Let it loose. It will defend itself."* My Heavenly Father is my **Truth.**

But I do understand that you might have disbelief, and you might question my actions. You are not alone. I also had the hardest time accepting that I was gifted in this way. The supernatural gift that God has gifted me with is beyond human imagination. The gift that God has gifted me came with blessings, but it also came with many hardships. It is a gift that caused people to see me as a liar, child of Satan, and a girl with mental problem. Many times, when I forget to count the blessing, it feels as if there are more hardships than blessings. If I am crazy, however, I am crazy and drunk with the anointed fire of the Holy Spirit.

As I said before, I did not "truly" know God until I was thirteen years old, when I was first anointed by the Holy Spirit and was given this supernatural gift. I was sixteen years old when I finally begin to leave my pride, my selfishness and accept what my Heavenly Father gave me as a gift. I have no reason to brag about my spiritual gift; it was not developed by my human capacities. The glory and praise go to our Heavenly Father.

In 1 Corinthians 12, we are introduced to many different spiritual gifts. Spiritual gifts are given by the indwelling of the Spirit of God; they are gifts of the Spirit. All believers have the indwelling of the Spirit. Believers cannot say that they have no gifts of the Spirit. God has given every believer a spiritual gift; all gifted differently, but every believer has one *(Romans 8:9)*. I learn in these past 5 years that, our spiritual gifts are to guide us closer to God, our Heavenly Father. They help us get to know Him and have closer relationship with Him.

In the past five years that I spent with God, the very first things I learn was how to trust, have faith, and believe in Him through hard times. I had to leave my pride, selfishness, and bitterness to carry my own cross and follow Jesus Christ *(Luke 14:27)*. It took me a while to realize that earthly ways are not God's way *(Isaiah 55:8)*. The moment I accepted the Lord as my savior, my life is no longer mine. My life is His; it has always been His.

I can no longer live without God's love. The contentment, peace, and joy that fill my heart each day are from the Heavenly Father. The thirst to get to know Him and the desperation to always be in His presence, the need to understand Him even more is in my blood now. The many days that I spend with Him no longer seem strange to me. The miracles in my life and anointed fire that fill me up every day no longer scare me; instead, I feel joy and love. I no longer look for the approval of others, nor do I wish to fit in with society. Now I look for my Father's approval. I wish to be His humble, loyal, and faithful servant.

Childhood

I was a quiet child, had very little friends and was always in my own little bubble. During my early childhood, my family and I lived with my father's side of the family, as was the tradition in Myanmar for the wife to live with the husband parents. I have three older brothers, and the cousins on my father's side were all boys too. I couldn't always tag along with them; they didn't always want to look out for me either. This meant I played by myself most of the time. My mother was my only best friend. I stuck by my mother and was called my mother's "pigtail" - I went wherever she went.

As a child, I was quite different from the other girls in my country. I would rather go with my mother and grandmother to their prayer meetings than play outside with kids my age. I would spend hours and hours playing by myself than with my classmates. I loved dressing up and dreamed of being a doctor, teacher, housewife, or crime investigator. I never dreamed about becoming a disciple of Jesus Christ. I had created a life plan at the age of 10 years old. I was going to finish high school, major in Medical, get a degree, travel around the world with my mother and become a successful woman without a worry in the world. I wanted to attain a certain level of confront and stability for my family, especially my mother. I had plans but the reality is, God messes up the plans that I had set at the age of ten years old. And that's a really good thing. I might complain, cry and yell at God more than I should but I loved the Lord. I trust the Lord and have faith in Him. I know that He has the best plan for me.

When I was six years old, my family moved away from my father's side of the family, to Yangon, Burma. We were getting ready to come to America, where my father and my mother sisters' families were already living. My father had left to go to America when I was 6 years old. We lived in Yangon, Burma for two years before we came to the United State. My mother introduced my brothers and I to a revival Pentecostal church called City Church. She did whatever she could to help us become closer to God. My mother took my brothers to a fasting prayer group every Saturday; she took us to prophets to get their blessings and have them lay their hands on each of us. She would ask Disciples of Christ to come and teach us about the Bible. Looking back, I realize that my life has always revolved around God.

When I was eight, we moved to the United States. I was very excited but very nervous. I didn't know at the time that a completely different world was waiting for me. When we first arrived, there was great excitement and expectations. I got to experience and see things that I have never seen before in Burma. But I was only living in a fool's paradise. My state of contentment and happiness did not last.

In March 2005, I started the second half of fourth grade with a trembling heart. I spoke little English and had no friends. I met people who looked nothing like me - they were tall and had different hair color and different facial structures. I had a hard time adjusting to the new culture. I was nothing like my classmates, and that made me very self-conscious.

The expectation I had about life in the United States was nothing like the reality that I faced. Chains of hardship also followed my family throughout the years. We had family and financial problems. We had no car, and my mom and oldest brother worked two to three jobs. My family of six lived in two-bedroom apartment. We all kept getting sick, and I went to the emergency room often because of a facial allergy that doctors couldn't diagnose. We had the toughest time in winter season.

As an eight-year-old, I couldn't understand how our lives had changed so much over the past couple of two months. My mother cried almost every night because of how tired emotionally and physically she was, and she wondered why she had decided to come to America. I was confused. Anger, bitterness, and sadness build up inside my heart. I felt that I was a volcano that could explode at any time.

At the age of ten, I developed depression. There were days when I would think about ways to kill myself. I couldn't find a reason to keep living; I didn't know why I was still living. I thought that feeling nothing would be better than feeling anger, bitterness, and loneliness. My relationship with my family was getting worse. I closed myself off from the world. I was no longer a bubbly, happy person. I kept to myself most of the time and had very little, if any, interaction with my family. The feeling of not belonging in this world was always in my heart. I was always waiting for something. I didn't feel complete - it was as if half of me wasn't there.

I began to rebel against my mother and didn't listen to her. I went out late at night and hang with the wrong crowd. I was trying to be someone that I wasn't, and that made me felt even worse. For a long time, loneliness was my only friend.

Summer of 2008

In the summer of 2008, my mother took me to a three-day revival crusade that was hosted by the church I attended in Frederick, Maryland. I went to church expecting nothing - I've been going to church my entire life, but I never felt anything from it. I went to church because my mother went to church and because I got to meet friends and so my mother wouldn't yell at me for not wanting to go to church.

I was a Christian in name only, I did not care much for God nor did I spend the time I needed with God. Of course, I went to church and attend Sunday Schools but the power of God, the importance of God did not truly register to me. Now that I am older and my relationship with God has grown, I've noticed the many mistakes I've made as a servant of God in the past. I had put my desires, my needs and my plans above the plans that He has for me.

So although I thought that this crusade would be like any other Sunday service, I went home with tears running down my face and with a yearning in my heart. It wasn't the guest pastor's preaching that blew me away, and it wasn't the people. Rather, it was the anointing fire of the Holy Spirit that begun to burn within me. I started crying, coming bare before God. I have never felt that naked; all my emotions that I've been hiding in my heart poured out. All the mistakes I'd made, things I didn't want to tell anyone - God knew it all. I didn't have to say it out loud for Him to hear it; He saw through my heart. My mother, who had experience with the work of Holy Spirit, said we should ask the guest preacher to pray for me, so we went up front and asked. He laid his hand on my head and prayed for me and left, but even then I was not satisfied. I was still crying, thirsty for something, but I didn't know what it was. The next day, my heart couldn't stay stilled. My whole body burned, asking me to pray and to ask for forgiveness, so that's what I did.

The reality of being a follower of Jesus Christ hit me full blown unprepared, but the reward waiting for me is better than anything else. I used to think that being gifted differently, standing up for my faith, and giving my heart fully to my heavenly Father was a shameful thing. Now, I stand here with confidence to tell you that there is nothing shameful about our God. I was saved. I was thirteen years old and was at the lowest point in my life. I couldn't handle all the emotions that were building up inside my heart. It had been three years since I first developed depression, and it was getting worse - I still couldn't find a reason to keep living. God knew I needed saving, and that's what He did.

My family and I went back to church in the evening on the second day of the crusade. That's when my first encounter with God began. I was filled with the anointed fire of the Holy Spirit. I couldn't stop crying; I finally had found my home. I felt peace coming over my body. I felt the burdens lifted off my shoulders.

The pastor from the crusade asked the church to come in front of the stage to pray together, and I went with two of my friends. I still remember praying from the bottom of my heart that I loved Him, that I needed Him in my life, and that I wanted to be filled with His presence. I said that I accepted everything that He was going to do in my life and that I was His. The moment I ended my prayer, I was overcome with the Holy Spirit. I fell straight down and lost consciousness. My soul and my whole body were taken over by the Holy Spirit. I had little control over my body - my body felt on fire and as if people were punching, hitting, and kicking me. I couldn't breathe, and I felt an overwhelming pain. I was scared, I asked for anyone to please take the pain away, and was saying "do you realized that every time you sin, you make me feel the pain of the crucifixion again?" I realized at that moment that the pain and the sadness I felt were all from Jesus' crucifixion day. I saw it all played out; it was like watching someone else going through it except that I was watching myself, not someone else. Jesus took my soul and said, "My child, ask forgiveness from people to whom you have done wrong. Don't let resentment and hurt keep controlling you."

I realized at that moment how important it is to forgive. When you don't forgive someone, you let that resentment control you. You can't move on or do things that God wants you to do without first letting resentment go. You won't be able to move forward or become closer to God without forgiveness and love. God won't be able to fully use you the way He wants to with all the restrictions you put on Him and yourself.

The pain and sadness that filled my entire body lasted for more than three hours. As I looked at my body and the people around me, something else caught my eye - the position in which my body lay. I was imitating the position in which Jesus was nailed on the cross. My feet were on top of each other, as if they were nailed together. My arms were outstretched, and my head sagged, as if all my energy was drained out. I should have been numb by the end of those three hours, but I wasn't. It was *His* miracle, not mine.

Everything was done with His power and His ability. I couldn't do anything. At midnight, the pastor asked my mother to take me home, as I was still overcome with the Holy Spirit; His work still was not done. My mother and brother carried me to the car because I still couldn't open my eyes. My eyes were closed for the entire time the event took place, much like Saul, who was blinded by the light of glory (*Acts* 9).

I remember the Holy Spirit telling my mother very important information in the car. The Holy Spirit said, "Your daughter is to be nailed on the cross for three days and three nights." The moment the Holy Spirit said that my mother begins to worry. Many questions ran through her mind in that short amount of time. "Was she to die too? This would bring so much shame to the family." The Lord knew what my mother was worried about because the next thing He said was. "Do you not trust me? Do you not trust the plans I have for my daughter? My child, you have to know the earthly ways are not my ways. Leave everything to me and trust me."

The Holy Spirit told my mother and brothers that they were to meet Him at four o'clock in the morning at the mountain to open my eyes. We all stayed up until four in the morning, and God was speaking to my family, teaching each one of us until it was time for us to meet him at the mountain. When we reached the mountain, we prayed until there was a flashing light in my vision, and I heard a voice say, "May God be with you forever and ever."

I opened my eyes, and for the first time that night, I had full control over my body. Those past eight hours that I'd spent with the Lord were my most peaceful and happiest moment. I learned that He is a God, a father, who knows everything about us. There is none like Him. His presence is full of joy, peace, kindness, compassionate, understanding and most of all, love. His love for us is unconditional.

Another thing I learned during those eight hours is that God want us to have a personal relationship with Him. We sometime have a relationship with God through others, but that's not what God wants. I also use to have a relationship with God through others. I had listen to others instead of taking heed to His voice. I had asked preachers and God servants to pray for me instead of praying to Him myself. Although there was nothing wrong with asking others to pray for you, I was not holding a deep, intimate relationship with God. I had put earthly things before God, but that's not what God wants. He desires each of us to have a personal relationship with Him and to love Him with all our hearts, with all our souls and mind. God wants us to put Him first in our lives (*Matthew 22:37*).

The first few months of my journey with God were filled with the anointing fire of the Holy Spirit. I walked in faith, but as a new believer, I knew very little about hardships that come with being a follower of Jesus Christ.

I begin as a prophet, but only a few people trusted what I had to say. Some had a hard time trusting my words because I was thirteen years old. Some didn't want to believe that God would use a girl who came from a broken and lower class household.

At thirteen years old, I was naive and gullible. I had lack wisdom and knowledge. I trusted people very easily and would follow others without any opinion. There were many mistakes I made in the beginning for not listening to God. At the time, I thought that all Christians had the same faith and beliefs. I later realized that is not true. Others trust in God but do not believe in Holy Spirit or speaking in tongue. Some forget God and place earthy entertainment and money above Him. We need to accept *Jesus, God the Father, and the Holy Spirit.* We cannot grow spiritually without all three of them.

In the beginning, I knew very little about what it meant to work for God. In the past, pastors or evangelical would mostly teach on repentance, salvation and blessings yet no one at the time taught us about how to live as a child of God. I depended on people, which isn't wrong but when it comes to our faith, we never should; this was a lesson I learned the hard way. I tried to meet people's expectations and tried too hard create the perfect life and faith that others were showing. I was not listening to the voice of

God or what God wanted me to do. I had put other's voices before God's voice.

Close to the middle of July 2008, I had followed God's servants to Canada to share my testimony with others. Those few weeks of staying in Canada were an eye opening moment for me. I realized that I had lots to learn and needed to spend more personal time with God. I begin to take in all of my past mistakes and asked for forgiveness. I loved God with all my heart, but I was listening to others' voices instead of His. That was one of the biggest mistakes I made. I used to think that being a follower of God was about having no hardship, being rich with materialistic things, and doing whatever I wanted to do, but I was wrong.

"He must become greater and greater; I must become less and less" - John 3:30

(12.13.10)

> **"He must become greater; I must become less"** - *John 3:30*

For a long time I honestly thought that I was the main lead in this story. I thought that because He loves me, I didn't have to obey Him or be afraid of Him. You can love God, but if you do not obey Him and respect Him, than the relationship you have with Him means nothing. There would be no difference between before and after you become born again. I thought that I could sin again and again and be forgiven, because He is a forgiving God. So many times, we take advantage of that. It is true that He is a forgiving and loving God, but we do not have the right to take advantage of that; we cannot continue to live the sinful life that we built before we knew God. It is true that God is with us but are we with Him? Ask yourself this question right at this moment. Do we set Him above everything else on earth? Do we fully trust in Him?

In August 2008, I closed myself away from God. I wanted to take a break from being a servant of God. When I arrived back from my trip to Canada, I became separated and disconnected from God. I felt that the people I had trusted weren't making me become a better person or help me become closer to God. I found myself becoming angry and disappointed in myself. But I learned that it was not my choice to decide whether or not I should take a break. The decision was His. Even though I thought that His work for me was done, God wasn't done with me yet.

On November 2008, I was gifted with the gift of tongue. My love for God was beginning to start growing rapidly again, and I had no doubts about any of His plans for me. I accepted everything He planned for my life because I knew that His plans always were better than the plans I had for myself.

Why?

*"I will proclaim the name of the Lord; how glorious
is our God!" - Deuteronomy 32:3*

The writings on my arms first appeared on December
14,2008 and stopped on December 14,2012. In those five
years, the people around me were amazed, fascinated, and
surprised. They asked me how the writings came to be on
my arms - some believed and some didn't, and that's okay.
They asked if it hurt or how many writings appeared on my
arms in a day, but none asked the reason or the message
behind the writings.

As a thirteen-year-old, I couldn't understand why the
writings on my arms surprised some people. To me, it wasn't
very surprising; instead, I was amazed by the power of God
and His glory. We all should know how powerful and mighty
our heavenly Father is, especially with the supernatural and
miracles that God showed in the Bible. God has the power
to gift me with the writings on my arms. Did the servants of
God not preach about the power of God and the crucifixion
of Jesus around the world? So why did Christians around

me choose to limit God's power and didn't limit Satan's. Why did they not apply their teaching to themselves?

When I started writing this book, I thought that God would tell me to write everything about the writing on my arms, but He didn't. Instead, the words that God gave me to write are the message behind each writings on my arms and why He gave me the gift.

I want to share with you the teaching that God taught me, the miracles that God has shown me, and the messages behind the writings on my arms.

"Don't let anyone think less of you because you are young. Be an example to all believers in what you say, in the way you live, in your love, your faith, and your purity." – 1 Timothy 4:12

(1.8.2010) and (11.30.2011)

The Gift

"I tell you the truth, anyone who believes in me
will do the same works I have done,
And even greater works, because I am going to be
with the Father" - John 14:12

When August came around, I went back to school. I thought
that my work for God was only a "summer thing" and that
God must be done with me. But He had greater plans for
me. On the morning of December 14,2008, I woke up
with a burning sensation on both of my arms. I was half
awake, trying to examine my arms, but found nothing.
There weren't any bruises or marks; it was the only burning
sensation that went all the way up my arms, and I had this
funny feeling in the middle of my chest.

I went back to sleep once more, not knowing what was
coming for me. What felt like a minute or two later I went
to sleep; the same burning sensation was overcoming both
my arms. I panicked and frantically looked at my arms, and
I saw the writings on my arms - an image of a rising sun
and the Hebrew letters that spelled "God." Freaking out,

I touched the writing and tried to remember everything I'd done the night before - anything that could've made these letters appear. But nothing extraordinary stood out from last night. I got out of bed and looked for my mom, who was at the gym at the time. When she arrived home, I immediately asked her to please come with me to my room. "I have something to show you," I said.

I wasn't scared. I was confused, but I was not scared. My whole being told me that I had nothing to worry about and that this was from my heavenly Father. When I showed the writing on my arms to my mom, she said, "Did you get a tattoo yesterday without telling me?"

With a bewildered expression, I said, "Of course not. I'm underage. I couldn't get a tattoo without a parent's permission." I explained to her the burning sensation I'd felt around my arms and the tingling coming from inside my heart.

She said, "We have to pray." At this point, it seemed we both had lost our minds. This was the first time that we'd ever experienced something like this, and we didn't quite know what to do. The first person my mother told about the writings on my arms was her older sister. We were worried, and my mother was scared, but I was just confused. An overwhelming peace and joy filled me, and I had no doubt that this gift was from God.

My mother and I ran to my aunt's house, which was next door to ours. She was in the shower, and we both knocked on the bathroom door and asked her to please come out because we had something very important to show her. She came out with a towel wrapped around her and a look of panic on her face. "What happen?" she asked us.

My mother explained about my arms, and I showed her. My aunt ran her hand across my arms and prayed. I think we must have all looked like deer caught in headlights. We didn't quite know what to do; we were new to the work of the Holy Spirit. So we did the only thing we knew to do, which was to go on with our day. We got ready to go to church, but I told my mother that we could not show the world my arms yet. We decided to wrap bandages around my arms, and the funniest part is that we never looked at my arms for the rest of the day to see if the writing was still there or had changed.

In the evening, my aunt called us and told us to come to her house to meet the prayer group, so that they could bless me. December 14, 2008, was the day God wrecked my life.

Praise

"For this, O Lord, I will praise you among the nations; I will sing praises to your name."
- 2 Samuel 22:50

My aunt often held a prayer group in the basement of her house, where her friends and all those who wanted to pray would come together. There were no restrictions on how to pray. Those who are blessed with other tongues would pray with other tongues, some danced, and some cried their heart out. I used to look at them and imagine God smiling down on them as they praised and worshipped Him.

I don't think anyone should stand still to praise God. He deserves all the praise in world. I don't think any of us can truly imagine what it was like for Jesus when He died for our sins. He suffered terribly for the people He loved. His sacrifice and out resulting salvation should fill us with joy.

If you feel like standing up, dancing, crying, and singing out loud in front of your fellow Christians, then do it. There is no shame in praising God. Of course, everyone's praise is different; so don't worry about how other people praise God. It doesn't matter as long as you praise your Lord Jesus Christ. You have been saved! Praise the Lord, now and forever!

First Meeting

"For I know the plans I have for you, declares the Lord, plans for welfare and not for evil, to give you a future and a hope" - Jeremiah 29:11

I went to my aunt house for the prayer meeting with a nervous heart and shaky legs. I did not know the plans that God has for me. As I went downstairs to the basement, I heard the prayer group praying, and an overwhelming feeling came out of my heart - it was as if my heart was going to explode. I thought it was because I was nervous, and told myself to calm down.

Everything I thought I knew about my life was going to change. No longer would I live for myself but rather for Him. Some people might not understand that sentence and might think I'm foolish for living my life for someone other than myself but how can I not be happy living for a God who so willingly gave His one and only Son - who was beaten, nailed to the cross, and belittled by the people around Him - because of my sins? His actions are very simple and easy to understand but some choose to make God a calculus problem. *Matthew 18:3* says, *"Truly I tell you, unless you change and become like little children, you will never enter the kingdom of heaven."* Little children have special humbleness and are easily taught, but most adults are not this way. Children, especially very young children, do not desire authority, do not regard outward distinction, are teachable, and willingly dependent on their parents. Most adult are different. They constantly compare their lives with others. Adults tend to worry more about money, earthly entertainment and their own desires then anything else. We must renew our minds to become simple and humble, as little children. As humans, it is impossible to be like little children, but with God, all things are possible. One must give control, meditate in the words of God and let God take control.

I knew my life was His the moment He saved me in the summer of 2008. He shined His light in the darkness that surrounded me and showed me the way out. When I went down to my aunt's house that evening, I expected nothing. I thought that we would pray, and the handwriting would be gone by night - I would fall asleep and wake up as If nothing had happened. But of course, God always seems to have other plans that have nothing to do with ours.

When we all were praying, the tingling feeling came back, but this time, it spread through out my entire body. As I felt this burning sensation, everyone was overcome with the anointed fire of the Holy Spirit. My head got heavier, and I felt as if I might lose consciousness, as if I was fainting, but I wasn't dizzy or weak. It was as if the Holy Spirit was fighting me to control my body, so I let myself go. I knew I had no reason to be scared. I didn't know what this was or what was going to happen to me, but I had faith in God. I want to use this experience as an example for our lives.

Every day, we try to control our lives, forgetting that we don't have the strength or the power to control anything. God gives us the freedom to choose, but He wants us to choose Him at the end of the day. He wants to willingly come to Him and give our lives to Him. That is as simple as it gets. When you choose Him, your life is no longer in your hands. You learn to put your life in His hands and trust Him every step of the way. He will cover your heart, guard you with His body, and love you with His heart. You'll find out that with God, nothing is impossible. When you accept His love and have faith in Him, you'll no longer have anything to fear because nothing in this world really matters. Your real home is with Him. When you give your life and your heart to Him, he'll never let you fall.

When I let go of my control and let the Holy Spirit have full control, He took me to a place I never could have imagined. Now, two things happened when I was taken. The first was that my spirit and soul were taken to heaven as the Holy Spirit overtook my body.

The first time I was taken to heaven was the evening in my aunt's basement with the prayer group. I remember being overcome with the Holy Spirit and God taking my soul away. I remember praying to God on the first day of the three-day crusade that I would serve him with all that I am. When I gave God that promise, I meant it with all my heart and have never been unhappy to fulfill it.

Remember, I am writing of these events through the eyes of my thirteen-year-old self. On the evening of December 14, 2008, I remember my soul being taken to heaven. It felt as if I was being transported. Two beautiful angels, wearing all white, brought me to a golden gate. In front of that golden gate, waiting for me, was Abraham. He had long beard and wore one of the most beautiful golden robes I'd ever seen. He had an aura of love. He gave me his hand, and as I took it, it seemed to electrify my arms.

Throughout all the time I was in heaven, I was calm. I wasn't scared. I knew that God was with me and that I was nowhere near harm. Abraham took me to a white room and said to me, "My child, the time is almost here. Follow the words of God. Live and breathe every word. My child, do not be scared of anything. Look only at the face of God and let His light guides you." Then the two angels took me to hell for a short time. The first thing I noticed, as we get closer to hell was the burning fire. I heard the people screaming, asking me to help them. I remember seeing the pain on their faces as they asked me for water and to take them out of the fire. They all kept asking for forgiveness. In my thirteen years, it was the first time I'd seen something so disturbing, so painful. I closed my eyes, cried and asked the angels to please take me away from there.

The angel on my left said, "Open your eyes, my child. What do you see?" I opened my eyes and looked around and saw horrible beasts - strong and big- everywhere. Some of the beasts were carrying people out of the cell and throwing them into the fire. The beasts were laughing, finding enjoyment in the humans' cries and screamed in the pit of fire. I was scared, even with the two angels by my side. I couldn't understand why some people thought there was no such thing as hell when it was right there in front of me. This place was completely different from heaven.

The angel on my right said, "My child, do not be scared. The beasts cannot touch you. We are here, always protecting you." As soon as the angel had finish talking, I felt them let go of my hands that they were holding. I felt myself falling into hell, screaming my lungs out and crying. As soon as the angels left my side, I've never been burned, but this pain, which was all over my body was a pain that I would never want to feel again. It was as if I was dropped into a wildfire, you can't get out but you can't die either. All I felt in hell was fear, pain, and sadness. The feeling of fire and fear were eating every part of my body, and I couldn't escape. My throat felt very dry, I couldn't breathe properly. The emotions I felt were completely different from the emotions I felt in heaven. Every part of my body was burning, but this fire wasn't going to let me die. You breathe through all the pain, but no one will come to help you.

When the angels came back, my body immediately felt at peace again and all the pain I had felt before disappeared. The angels then said, "You have to go back. Do not be afraid. Trust in God and only God. Look only at Him, and hold His hand through every hardship to come. Do not give into temptation. The time is almost here." As soon as the angels finished speaking, my soul instantly went back to my body. I was confused, not only by the things I was experiencing but also by the reason why God chose me, out of all the people in the world, for this gift. When I opened my eyes again, I was back in my aunt's basement.

"One day the Pharisees asked Jesus, "When will the Kingdom of God come?" Jesus replied, "The Kingdom of God can't be detected by visible signs. You won't be able to say, 'Here it is!' or 'It's over there!' For the Kingdom of God is already among you." Then he said to his disciples, "The time is coming when you will long to see the day when the Son of Man returns,[c] but you won't see it. People will tell you, 'Look, there is the Son of Man,' or 'Here he is,' but don't go out and follow them. For as the lightning flashes and lights up the sky from one end to the other, so it will be on the day when the Son of Man comes. But first the Son of Man must suffer terribly and be rejected by this generation. "When the Son of Man returns, it will be like it was in Noah's day. In those days, the people enjoyed banquets and parties and weddings right up to the time Noah entered his boat and the flood came and destroyed them all. "And the world will be as it was in the days of Lot. People went about their daily business—eating and drinking, buying and selling, farming and building— [29] until the morning Lot left Sodom. Then fire and burning sulfur rained down from heaven and destroyed them all. Yes, it will be 'business as usual' right up to the day when the Son of Man is revealed." – Luke 17:20-30 (3.25.2011)

The Bride

"Let us rejoice and be glad and give Him glory! For the wedding of the Lamb has come, and his bride has made herself ready. Fine linen, bright and clean, was given her to wear. Then the angel said to me, "Write this: Blessed are those who are invited to the wedding supper of the Lamb! And he added, these are the true words of God." - Revelation 19:7-9

When my soul was taken to heaven, the Holy Spirit overtook my body. I sat on a sofa at the front of the basement room, and I had an elegance that I never could have mastered at age thirteen.

The Holy Spirit had told the people in the room to make me wear a white dress. They all wondered where they could get a white dress, as no one seemed to own a white dress, and I didn't have one either. The Holy Spirit, however, knew that my aunt had a white dress that my older cousin had worn as a flower girl from years ago.

My aunt went upstairs to get the dress for me, and after I put it on and sat on the sofa, the Holy Spirit asked the prayer group to look at me. My skin was glowing, and there were no blemishes on my body. The person who sat on that sofa at the front of the room looked nothing like me. She was beautiful and spoke with a soft voice, but each word held strong power. Wisdom, love, and righteousness radiated within her. The prayer group looked at her - at me - but none of them understood at the time why the Holy Spirit had asked me to dress in white. We did not understand the message behind that day until three months later.

So what does it mean to be the bride of Jesus Christ? Christ, who is perfect, will have a perfect bride. This does not mean perfect in an earthly way but rather in spiritually. The bride will have to get ready, but she cannot be made ready without Christ's help. *Ezekiel 16* tells us that God washed, dresses, and blessed the nation of Israel so that she would be prepared to be His wife. He cleansed her, groomed her, and dressed her in royal garments - he prepared her. But first, we must ask for God's help. As humans, we tend to let our pride get in the way of our faith. We see only the things that are visible and have only faith in the things that are seen. It would be hard to ask God and surrender to Him with our human faith, so we must have supernatural faith.

> "Later I passed by, and when I looked at you and saw that you were old enough for love, I spread the corner of my garment over you and covered your naked body. I gave you my solemn oath and entered into a covenant with you, declares the Sovereign Lord, and you became mine. I bathed you with water and washed the blood from you

and put ointments on you. I clothed you with an embroidered dress and put sandals of fine leather on you. I dressed you in find linen and covered you with costly garments. I adored you with jewelry: I put bracelets on your arms and a necklace around your neck, and I put a ring on your nose, earring on your ears and a beautiful crown on your head. So you were adored with gold and silver; your clothes were of fine linen and costly fabric and embroidered cloth. Your food was honey, olive oil and finest flour. You become very beautiful and rose to be a queen. And your fame spread among the nations on account of your beauty, because the splendor I had given you made your beauty perfect, declares the Sovereign Lord." - Ezekiel 16:8-14

Think of Christ, doing the same exact thing for us, but in the most magnificent way, preparing us spiritually. God is not preparing us physically, but spiritually, to be with Him in the holy place - heaven. *Ezekiel 16:8-14* says that *the bride of Christ will be adorned in fine linen, clean and white -* meaning that the bride of Christ will be the perfect, spiritual bride - with righteousness of Christ upon her.

So why was I radiant in love, wisdom, and righteousness? Some of the most repeated words in the handwriting on my arms were love, peace, and wisdom. When you have God as your father, Jesus Christ inside you and the Holy Spirit as your guide, you will only feel love and peace. You will know that no matter what hardship you are experiencing, He will always be there for you, guiding you, and fighting with you through all the pain. He will be the light to lead you out of the darkness. Love and peace naturally comes from God. Wisdom and righteousness are the most important parts of growing with God.

"But by His doing you are in Christ Jesus, who became to us wisdom from God, and righteousness and sanctification, and redemption" - 1 Corinthians 1:30

Being the bride of Jesus Christ isn't about standing at the altar in a white dress or how pretty you look. It's about waiting and preparing for His presence in your life on a daily basis and focusing on your relationship with Christ.

While on earth, we worry about the physical parts of the wedding and a lot of time - we simply get married because we like the idea of becoming married. God will not look at those things. Christ will look at our hearts. He will be looking at whether or not we only look at Him. He is a God who does not care for the outer appearance but rather the inner beauty.

Waiting for anything in life is quite difficult, but the waiting is important to becoming followers of God. To wait for God means that we put our hearts and souls into being prepared for Him and His calling on our lives.

The most important message behind the writings on my arms with which God gifted me was that He is coming soon. Are you ready? Have you prepared yourself to be the bride of Jesus Christ? You are called to be Jesus Christ's bride. Sadly, not every engagement ends in a successful trip to the alter. So how do we prepare ourselves for presentation to our spiritual bridegroom, Jesus Christ?

Preparing to be the Bride of Jesus Christ

"The wedding of the Lamb has come, and His bride has made herself ready." - Revelation 19:7

I used to think that if I was saved and was a Christian, then I would go to heaven. But when God taught me about the process of being a disciple of Christ and prepared me to be the bride of Jesus Christ, I realized that reaching heaven wasn't as easy as I thought it would be. Did you know that not all "Christians" will go to heaven? I learned about the Bride of Jesus Christ at the age of fifteen years old, the Lord told me that not everyone who professes to be a Christian will be counted among those spend eternity in heaven with the heavenly Father. I'm not the one who came up with this idea; I'm telling you exactly as the Lord told me. This idea originated with Jesus Christ.

"Not everyone who says to me, 'Lord, Lord,' will enter the kingdom of heaven, but only the one who do the will of my father who is in heaven.

Many will say to me on that day, 'Lord, Lord, did we not prophesy in your name and in your name drive out the demons and in your name perform many miracles?' Then I will tell them plainly, 'I never knew you. Away from me, you evildoers!" - *Matthew 7:21-23*

The above verses tell us that not everyone who calls Jesus "Lord" will enter into the kingdom of heaven. So what get us into heaven? According to *Matthew 7:21*, only those who do the will of God will enter into the kingdom of heaven. We must be spirit-filled, word-filled, holy, radiant, and blameless. We must live a life of righteous acts and sincerely be devoted to Jesus Christ. *Ephesian 2:10* tell us that we are created in Jesus Christ to do good works. He is the potter, and we are the clay. He molds us and makes us for His good purpose. *Proverbs 16:9* tell us that we might be planning our own plans, but it is the Lord who establishes our steps.

I can't tell you how to live your life as a Christian. Everyone is gifted differently and is called differently as well. In the very beginning of my journey, I thought that getting to know God through my pastors and other Christians was enough, but that's not what God desires for me. He desires for each of us to know Him personally. God wants us to spend alone time with Him, to mediate in the words of God and to have a personal relationship with Him.

It is hard to transform, even as Christians. I had the hardest time at the very beginning of my journey as a servant of God, because I felt that as child of God, I had to be perfect. Because I was trying so hard to be perfect, I became unhappy. I was disappointed in myself. I saw being a Christian and spending time with God as chores, but that's not what God is looking for. He doesn't need us to be perfect. Our definition of "perfect" is completely different from His definition of "perfect." We try to change, in our human ability, and put up a facade of happiness and bliss, pretending nothing bad ever happens. That's not what God wants. He wants us to come to Him just as we are and devote ourselves to Him. We don't even have to do anything. He'll transform us with the anointing power of the Holy Spirit. As we give to God and begin a loving relationship with Him, only then we will fulfill *Ephesians 5:25-27*:

> *"Husbands, love your wives, as Christ loved the church and gave himself up for her, that he might sanctify her, having cleansed her by the washing of water with the word, so that he might present the church to himself in splendor, without spot or wrinkle or any such thing, that she might be holy and without blemish" - Ephesian 5:25-27*

When talking about the "bride of Christ," some people think this refers to the church building, but the Bible is referring to the people in church - about the relationship we have with God while we are here on earth, a relationship that is so close and spiritually intimate that only the best imagery is of bride and groom.

Christ, the bridegroom, has lovingly chosen His bride in *Ephesian 5:25-27* but just as a bride and a groom are separated until the wedding, so is the bride of Christ separate from her bridegroom. The bride's responsibility during the betrothal is to be faithful to Him. The church will be united with the bridegroom at the second coming of Christ, the official "wedding ceremony." As believers, we who are the bride of Jesus Christ must wait with anticipation for the day when we will unite with our groom but until then we must remain faithful to Him and not be swayed by the earthly things in this universe.

Then how should we prepare ourselves as God's bride? To be the bride of Jesus Christ, we must first surrender our heart to Him. If we continuously allow our heart to be filled with earthly things than where will God reside in our heart? We have to clear our heart of things from this world and open the door for the Lord to enter. We must submit ourselves daily to the Word of God, pray daily and ask the Lord to give us the strength to resist any temptations that come our way. *Revelation 19:7-8 says, "Let us rejoice and be glad and give him glory! For the wedding of the lamb has come and His bride has made herself ready. Fine linen, bright and clean, was given her to wear."*

The "ready" bride of Christ is characterized by righteous acts. The bride of Christ puts her faith into practice; she applies it to every part of her daily life. *Second Corinthians 11:2-3* says that the bride of Christ, this "pure virgin", is ready for presentation to Jesus, the bridegroom. She is characterized by "sincere pure devotion to Christ," *Matthew 22:37-38* tell us to keep the first and greatest commandment - to love the Lord our God with all our hearts.

Are we on God side?

There is a quote by Abraham Lincoln that I love and always ask myself in any situation that I am in. During the Civil War, Lincoln was asked if God was on his side. "Sir, my concern is not whether God is on my side," replied the president. "My greatest concern is to be on God's side, for God is always right." Are we doing what God wants us to do, or are we doing what we want God to want us to do? There is a huge difference. The world that we are living in now is different than the world that we were living in a year ago. The world has become scarier and scarier. We begin to live in the world's expectation, we become slaves of the world but we must remember that our world isn't a godly world, our world is own by Satan. Many temptations and trials come our way, but we must stand firm and have faith in God. *1 Corinthians 9:24-27* says, *"Do you not know that in a race all the runners run, but only one gets the prize? Run in such a way as to get the prize. Everyone who competes in the games goes into strict training. They do it to get a crown that will not last, but we do it to get a crown that will last forever. Therefore I do not run like someone running aimlessly; I do not fight like a boxer beating the air. No, I strike a blow to my body and make it* my slave so that after I have preached to others, I myself will not be disqualified for the prize." We must discipline ourselves to get to the finish line, where our heavenly Father is waiting for us with a prize. Remember, it is not how we begin that matters; it is the end of the journey that matters.

Mountain

"One of those days Jesus went out to a mountainside to pray and spent the night praying to God" - Luke 6:12

In the earliest days of my walk with God, the mountainside was my best friend. I would wake up early in the morning, and either my mom or my brother would drive me to the mountain. There, I would find the alone time I needed with God. Some of my most precious moments with God were spent in the wilderness, where the sound of the wind blowing through the trees was my only companion. I loved going up to the mountain and finding shelter in the arms of my heavenly Father, but waking up was always hard for me.

Some days, I would wake up okay, but other days I would wake up grumpy. My mother would have dragged me out of bed, bundle me up, and drive up to the mountain. But I soon fell in love with the cold air and welcomed it every winter. Waking up before sunrise became a habit.

I have to tell you, though, that I didn't choose to wake up in the morning and drive to the mountain, nor did I ever think that I needed the alone time with God. It all started with God telling me to meet Him at the mountain. I never regretted it.

My first visit was on the very day that God decided to "wreck" my life - in the summer of 2008. As I was overcome with the anointing fire of the Holy Spirit, an intense light blinded my eyes. My mouth was moving, but the words that came out were from the Holy Spirit. I could hear the voices of others who surrounded me, but at the same time, I felt far away. I could not open my eyes during the entire time that I experienced the Holy Spirit.

The experience I had at church started around nine o'clock at night and ended at midnight. My mother and brothers had to carry me out of church, as I could not open my eyes at all. On the ride home, the Holy Spirit told my mother and brothers that I was to meet God at the mountain at four o'clock in the morning. We all stayed up the whole night, and God spoke to each one of my family members. The spoken words held so much power. My mother said, "In each word that He spoke, I could hear the love He has for us all. Each word was spoken with elegance and status. His power radiated in each word."

When my mother, my brother, a family friend and I went to the mountain at four in the morning, an overwhelming peace came over my entire body. I knew I was in the presence of my heavenly Father. I started praying, and as I prayed, I heard the most smoothing voice; it spoke with such kindness and love. "My princess, open your eyes," the voice said. "Keep my words close to your heart and have faith."

As I opened my eyes, I looked up at the sky and saw the brightest moon I'd ever seen, shining down on where we were standing. That morning started my love for the moon. I had never looked at the sky or been in awe by it, but since I started my walk with God, I have seen the beauty of the world He created. Every day, I am amazed by the love that He has for us. My first visit to the mountain was the first time I personally heard the voice of God, but it was also the first time I experienced the presence of Satan.

In the beginning I couldn't feel Satan's presence. I did not even know that Satan was with in our group. It was only until after God spoke to me that I notice his presence. He had been eavesdropping from afar, as he could not come near me. He was watching my every move carefully and listening to my every word, not because he wants to listen but because he needed to twist it around. As humans, we need to know that we are living in a world where Satan is freely roaming around, trying to find his next victim. We always have to be on our guard and need God to protect us throughout every second and minute of the day.

My second visit took place at the beginning to the winter season. Early mornings are colder then, and the darkness stays a little longer. All I wanted to do was snuggle up in bed, sleep a little longer, and never step out of the house. So waking up at four in the morning to go to the mountain, where it is colder than in the city, made me grumpy. As usual, I woke up because God woke me up. I couldn't ignore Him. He would tell me the specific time He wanted us to meet Him. I would go to the mountain with an angry face, but I always came back down with an excited heart and happy face.

On that particular morning, two of my mother's friends, who are also in the prayer group, came with us. When we got to the mountain, we went our separate ways to pray. I saw a tree stump in the middle of the ground, so I knelt on top of the stump and began praying.

As I prayed, an intense light overcame my eyes again, and I felt a burning sensation over my entire body - I was already familiar with this feeling. As I continue to pray, I felt peace and joy overcome my body. As I connected with God, my mother saw that there was a glow around my arms - she saw it and I felt it. My heavenly Father said to me, "My princess, there is nothing to be afraid. I am with you always." The moment He said that, my heart found an overwhelming peace and happiness in the light.

I looked up at the sky again and saw thousands of stars shining brightly; they all were grouped above me. These beautiful stars, shining brightly in the darkness, seemed to say, *You're safe. There is no darkness that the light won't shine through.*

In the many years that I spent with God, I accepted that there is *nothing* that He cannot do. He is powerful, forever-loving, and forgiving God. He could have chosen anyone in the world, yet He took the time to notice someone like me and present me with a gift that no one else had. I'm not the most colorful crayon or the most beautiful, nor am I the kindest person in the world, but He chose to love me - not because I please Him but because He simply loves me. He has shown me so many miracles that are hard to believe, but I know my God. I know how powerful and loving He is. Many of us forget sometimes that He created heaven and earth. We forget that the God in the Old Testament is the same God in the New Testament.

First Love

"Love is patient, love is kind. It does not envy, it does not boast, it is not proud. It is not rude, it is not self-seeking, it is not easily angered, and it keeps no record of wrong. Love does not delight in evil but rejoices with the truth. It always protects, always trusts, always hopes, and always preservers. Love never fails. But where there are prophecies, they will cease; where there are tongues, they will be stilled; where there is knowledge, it will pass away." - 1 Corinthians 13:4-8

Out of all the people that I know, my mother is the most kindest, loving and naive person that I've ever met. Sometime her words might be as sharp as knife but her words are full of honestly and love. She used to be my definition of love. Now, my definition of love is God. A friend of mine asked me if I love my mother more than my father. I responded that I love God more than my mother or father.

God is my first love. And that is the one thing God wants from us more than anything else. He wants us to love Him, not only in the good moments but also in the bad. Jesus once was asked which of God's commandments was the most important. Jesus answered immediately, *in Matthew 22:37, "The most important commandment is this: love the Lord your God with all your heart and with all your soul and with all your mind."* In the past five years, I learned that God wants us to put Him above everything else in our lives. When I went through my first trials as a Christian, I felt a bit of resentment against God. Looking back now, I can't say that I loved Him with all my heart. I loved Him to some degree but never succeeded in loving Him with all my being at every moment, as the command suggested we should.

I didn't quite understand what love was until I was in the presence of God. I am consumed by His love. In one of my many visits to heaven, I had the honor of meeting Jesus. At thirteen years old, I already had an image of Jesus. In my child's mind, He was fairy-tale prince. He was a charmer, sitting in His throne, showing little emotion. A commoner like me would never be able to reach Him.

When I got to finally meet Jesus, He was nothing like the way I painted Him in my mind. He was shining! He came closer to me and played with me. He radiated with love, kindness, wisdom, and glory. There were marks on His hands and feet. I was a bit scared and cautious, because I had never experienced this before.

Jesus said, "My child, there is nothing to be afraid of. I am here! You are safe." He held my right hand. I suddenly felt a tingling feeling all over my right arms. Jesus took me to a beautiful garden, filled with colorful flowers. The flowers all had bloomed so beautifully and big; there were no dead flowers. I ran around, asking Jesus to play with me. I was overcome with happiness and joy, just by simply being in His presence. For the first time in my life, I fell in love. Jesus is my first love.

Abraham

"Abram fell facedown, and God said to him, "As for me, this is my covenant with you: You will be the father of many nations. No longer will you be called Abram; your name will be Abraham, for I have made you a father of many nations. I will make you fruitful; I will make nations of you, and kings will come from you." - Genesis 17:3-6

Many of my visits to heaven occurred when I was thirteen years old. In every visit, Abraham was the first person I would meet. He would always wait for me in front of the golden gate, which is one of the golden entrances. Abraham had a loving and kind soul. I vividly remember his full beard.

I had a love/hate relationship with Abraham. I would get excited whenever I saw Abraham at the beginning of my visits, because that meant I was in heaven, but when I saw Abraham at the end of each visits, I was not happy, because I knew my visit was ending.

Sometimes I refused to go back on earth. I begged and pleaded with Abraham to let me stay. Abraham always had the same answer each time: "Child, it is not your time. Your Father has plans and purpose for you on earth."

And my reply also was always the same: "I'll come back and live here eventually, so why not let me stay now?" There were times when it became so difficult for me to leave that one time Abraham pushed me over. It felt as if I was falling down from a bridge, but I wasn't; I was just going back to earth. That very visit started my love and my dislike for Abraham.

Queen Esther

I met Queen Esther on one of my visit to heaven. She was the most beautiful person I have ever met. She was wearing the most beautiful gown and golden jewels. She also had a golden crown on her head. I could feel her inner strength and gentleness as soon as I was near her. She held my hand and guides me to a room decorated with the most beautiful gems. "Have strength in the Lord", she says, "For the harder days are coming."

Gabriel and Michael

"And the angel answered him, "I am Gabriel. I stand in the presence of God, and I was sent to speak to you and to bring you this good news." - Luke 1:19

"Now war arose in heaven, Michael and his angels fighting against the dragon. And the dragon and his angels fought back" - Revelation 12:7

On another of my visits to heaven, I met with Gabriel and Michael. Gabriel is a messenger, while Michael is a warrior. Gabriel has a strong but gentle soul. When I was in his presence, I felt peace, but I could tell that he was strong, spiritually and physically. Michael also has gentle soul, at least in my presence. They both had a very strong presence. I felt safe and guarded when I was next to the angels. Because I was thirteen years old, I didn't have many questions or any deep thoughts. I was a free-spirited child.

I knew I was safe; the feeling of happiness, joy, and peace always overcome me when I was in heaven. All the hardship and pain I went through on earth was forgotten. On many occasions, Michael would guard me. Gabriel would sometimes play with me in the garden or in the playground - there were many animals in the playground. I never really paid attention to the type of animals they were. As a child, I felt close to Michael and Gabriel since they always come to play with me.

God and Michael

"At that time the sign of the Son of Man will appear in the sky, and all the nations of the earth will mourn. They will see the Son of Man coming on the clouds of the sky, with power and great glory. And he will send his angels with a loud trumpet call, and they will gather his elect from the four winds, from one end of the heavens to the other." - Matthew 24:30-31

In one of my many visits to heaven, I was taken to a bright all-white room. In that room were Michael and God. Michael was wearing his warrior suit, as he was getting ready for war. And God - how magnificent His glory and power was in that room! Michael was turn toward me, while God had His back to me. I could not see His face but bright lights shone within and around Him.

God and Michael were having a deep conversation. I stood in the corner of the room, watching them. God knew I was in the room, as He said, "My princess, listen carefully. I am coming soon."

In my next visit to heaven, I was again in the bright all-white room with God and Michael. But this time, instead of having a deep conversation, Michael was on his way out of the room. God said to me, "My princess, Michael is gathering the army. I am coming!"

In my pervious visit, God had said He was coming soon, but on this visit, Michael was on his way out the door, gathering his army, and God said, "I am coming."

"*At that time Michael, the great prince who protects your people, will arise. There will be a time of distress such as has not happened from the beginning of nations until then. But at that time your people - everyone whose name is found written in the book - will be delivered*" - *Daniel 12:1*. The time has come! When we look around us, our world is slowly beginning to fall apart. We're turning away from God, choosing to do what we want instead of asking God. We forget that earth is not our home. The things we've worked hard for - money, fame, status - means nothing when we pass away. Prepare yourself for the second coming!

Crowns in Heaven

"For we must all appear before the judgment seat of Christ, so that each of us may receive what is due us for the things done while in the body, whether good or bad." - 2 Corinthians 5:10

On another visits to heaven, I was taken to a beautiful room; this room was full of people wearing different crowns. It felt as if I was in a king's house, everything in the room was gold. The room was decorated beautifully. In the room, some crowns had one diamond, while others had different colored crowns and more than one diamond. I asked the angel next to me why they wore crowns, why some wore crowns with more diamonds than others who only have one, and why the crowns had different colors. The angel said that each crown represented the rewards they'd received for the things they had done while in the body. The different colors represented the foundation on which they'd built their works.

"By the grace God has given me, I laid a foundation as a wise builder, and someone else is building on it. But each one should build with care. For no one can lay any foundation other than the one already laid, which is Jesus Christ. If anyone builds on this foundation using gold, silver, costly stones, wood, hay or straw, their work will be shown for what it is, because the Day will bring it to light. It will be revealed with fire, and the fire will test the quality of each person's work. If what has been built survives, the builder will receive a reward. If it is burned up, the builder will suffer loss but yet will be saved—even though only as one escaping through the flames."

(1 Corinthians 3:10–15)

The angel explained that there are five different crowns in heaven. When I asked which crown I would receive, the angel said the crowns and rewards of heaven that God promises are for those who are faithful to Him forever, only then would I know which crown I will receive. I told Him I would be forever faithful to my heavenly Father.

The angel then explained the meaning of each crown. The first heavenly crown is for those who are faithful until the very end, the imperishable crown.

The second crown is the crown of rejoicing. This crown is for those who lead others to Jesus Christ. The crown is also for those who demonstrate fruitfulness by influencing others toward righteousness.

The third crown is the crown of righteousness. This crown is inherited through the righteousness of Christ - without Christ's righteousness, we cannot obtain the crown. This crown is not for those who depend upon their own sense of righteousness or their own works.

The fourth crown is the crown of glory. The crown is awarded to those who long for or love His appearing. The word glory refers to the very nature of God and His actions. *"For I consider that the sufferings of this present time are not worthy to be compared with the glory which shall be revealed to us" (Romans 8:18)*

The fifth crown is the crown of life. This crown is for all believers, but it is mostly for those who endure sufferings, who were held captive and who bravely suffered persecution for Jesus, even to the point of death.

We know that earthly lives will end. But we have the amazing promise that comes only to those who came to God through Jesus. *"And this is the promise that He has for us - eternal life" (1 John 2:25).*

I asked the angel why some people in the room had more than one crown, and he answered, "Because they surrendered their lives in more than one way."

I lifted my head and felt that I had the crown of rejoicing and the crown of life. It fits exactly to my head and was made of gold and different designs. I knew I was wearing the crown, because it was very heavy. The angel looked at me and said, "My child, you must remain as a faithful disciple of Christ. Do not stray from the Lord. No matter what hardships and pains come your way, the Lord, your Father, already has won against them all." And again, I was taken back to earth.

My Princess

"You know when I sit and when I rise; you perceive my thoughts from afar. You discern my going out and my lying down; you are familiar with all my ways. Before a word is on my tongue you know it completely, O Lord." - Psalm 139:2-4

In my many visits to heaven and whenever I am alone with God, He calls me a name that I fell in love with, and that's "My princess." Isn't it funny how He knows each one of us? I used to imagine God sitting on His throne and looking down at earth, probably judging everyone and not really caring about us. I thought He would be like one of those cold-hearted kings. But He knows us! He knows our names and what we like and dislike.

God not only knows who you are, but He also knows where you are, and He knows what you're going through, why you're going through it, and how you feel. He knows you better than you know yourself. He cares about you personally.

On many occasions when I've felt discouraged or alone, God has always let me know He was there, with a Bible verse written on my arms. When I forget His love even for a second, He is quick to remind me. Before I even begin to pray or talk about a problem, God lets me know how to solve the problem, or He tells me that He knows, either through the writings on my arms or a visit from the Holy Spirit.

Isn't amazing that the most powerful living God, who created heaven and earth, would want sinful human beings like you and me? He wants a relationship with us! He is waiting for us to come home, to be with Him. Before I had a relationship with God, I had heard others talk about the home He created for us in heaven. I couldn't quite believe it until on my third visit to Heaven, I was taken to my home - a home that was made of gold. In my backyard, there was a big garden with endless blooming flowers, and there also was a swing that I would ride whenever I visited. There were an endless number of books in one of the rooms. I love reading but none of these books were of the romance or horror genre, which I enjoy; they were books of praise and worship, which I've been collecting here on earth. Each detail in my home was a part of me. Every interior or exterior design of the house was everything I've been wishing for. There also were golden rivers, and I was baptized in one of these rivers. Angels praised the Lord. Some played instruments, and some danced. I had endless amount of handmade gold clothes. Each piece of clothing was embroidered with different designs.

Whenever I was invited to eat with Jesus or meet with God, I often was called "My princess." (Don't forget each and every one of us is His precious child.) I sat on the left side of the table, and Jesus sat in the middle. I was served fish and fruits. Sitting there, having dinner in heaven, felt like a dream but a beautiful dream from which I wished I never had to wake up.

Soon, though, it won't be a dream. I will go back home, where my Father is waiting for me and where my first love is.

Holy Spirit

"But the Helper, the Holy Spirit, whom the Father will send in my name, he will teach you all things and bring to your remembrance all that I have said to you" - John 14:26

In the five years that I walked with God, the Holy Spirit was my best friend, my guide, and my teacher. Of all the gifts that God gave to me, none was greater than the presence of the Holy Spirit.

Just by having the Holy Spirit inside of me, I have an overwhelming happiness, and it feels as if my heart is about to burst. I love spending quiet time with Him, especially in the early mornings. When friends ask me why I spend so much time by myself, I tell them, "You wouldn't understand. I am not spending time alone. I am spending time with my heavenly Father, my first love, my teacher, and my best friend."

You can't find such happiness anywhere in the world. The Holy Spirit is the personal presence of God Himself. God is the Father, the Son, and the Holy Spirit. Now, this does not mean we worship three beings. Rather, we worship one God, who is the eternal triune within Him in three equal persons.

In these past five years, I learn that the Holy Spirit has many purposes, roles and activities. I've seen many, particularly pastors and evangelist, who think that the Holy Spirit is not important. Some Christians have a hard time believing in the work of the Holy Spirit but the Holy Spirit does work in the hearts of all people. You can't deny the Holy Spirit if you are a Christian. Jesus told His disciples in *John 16:7-11* that He would send the Holy Spirit into the world to *"convict the world of guilt in regard to sin and righteousness and judgment."*

When I surrendered my heart to God and let Him have full control in the summer of 2008, it was the Holy Spirit that takes up residence in my heart. It was through the Holy Spirit that God did His work in me. God send the Holy Spirit to us to be our helper, comforter, and guide. In *John 14:16*, Jesus says, *"And I will ask the Father, and He will give you another counselor to be with you forever."* Among Holy Spirit many functions, one is the Revealer of truth. The Holy Spirit's presence within us allows us to understand and interpret the words of God. When I first started studying the Bible, God told me to invite the Holy Spirit before I read the word of God, only then would I understand the truth. Jesus told His disciples in *John 16:13* that *"When He, the Spirit of Truth, comes, He will guide you into all truth."* Before I invited the Holy Spirit, the Bible felt like a foreign language to me but when I invite the Holy Spirit, the ultimate guide, the Bible become easier to understand and making all things plain and clear. The Lord ways, His plans become clear to me.

I'm not talking about this in earthly ways; rather He leads in the way we should go in all spiritual ways. Without such guide, we are likely to fall into temptations. My mother said the scariest thing in life is for the Holy Spirit to leave us. I've seen many pastors who were left by the Holy Spirit, not because He wanted to leave but because they made him leave. They would start with the word of God, anointed with the Holy Spirit, only to be blinded with money, status, earthly entertainment, or materialistic things.

Another one of the Holy Spirit's functions is that of gift-giver. This function is one of the most controversial subjects. Many people have a difficult time believing in spiritual gifts but what people don't realize is that we need those spiritual gifts to help us become closer to God. *First Corinthians 12* describes some of the spiritual gifts given to believers. So why did God give us spiritual gifts? *Ephesians 4:12-13,15* says that the gifts of the Holy Spirit were given "*to equip his people for works of service, so that the body of Christ may be built up until we all reach unity in the faith and in the knowledge of the Son of God and become mature, attaining to the whole measure of the fullness of Christ ...Instead, speaking the truth in love, we will grow to become in every respect the mature body of him who is the head, that is, Christ.*" Our heavenly Father distributes the gifts of the Holy Spirit among His children, so that we can glorify Him through the spiritual gifts. The Holy Spirit reveals Jesus' purpose for us. I feel that the purpose of my life - and yours too - is to glorify God through the power of the Holy Spirit and to love others and to spread the good news of the Lord. The Holy Spirit will reveal the finer details of our purpose and our plans for life as we study the word of God and walk in faith.

The Holy Spirit is also the fruit-producer in our lives. When we accept Jesus Christ into our lives, we receive salvation, forgiveness, and freedom - and the Holy Spirit, a gift promised by Jesus Christ himself. *Galatians 5:22-23* says that the fruit of the Spirit is *"love, joy, peace, forbearance, kindness, goodness, faithfulness, gentleness and self-control."* How is the Holy Spirit our fruit producer? The things Paul listed in *Galatians 5:22-23* are not produced by our best efforts. The fruit of the Spirit is the products of the Holy Spirit's presence in our life. We must believe, have faith and let God have full control; only then will we bear the spiritual fruit.

The Disciple God wants us to be

"Love the Lord your God with all your heart and with all your soul and with all your strength." -
Deuteronomy 6:5

In the early days of my walk with God, I often looked at the lives of other Christians and used them as my examples. Sometimes they didn't work out—as humans, we make mistakes, and as Christians, we try to cover up insecurities, pain, mistakes, doubts, and failures. We might bottle up our emotions and end up with anger and depression. We might blame God and have resentment. Some of us have an unhappy walk with God, while others pull themselves away from God. We set ourselves for failure when we look for the approval of others and present our faith as easier than it really is.

Whenever guest speakers would come to our church, they would speak about blessing after blessing—all materialistic. I would daydream and set my expectations of what being a Christian is like. While listening to each sermon, I promised myself that when I did find God, when the Holy Spirit anointed me, I would lead a life just like them.

In the summer of 2008, when I finally found God, I was anointed with the Holy Spirit. I was overcome with the Holy Spirit and reenacted scenes, from Jesus' praying in Gethsemane (Matthew 26:36-56) to Jesus' crucifixion (Matthew 27:33-44). I became a disciple of Jesus Christ with expectations, but what waited for me—temptations, trials, pain, and hardships—was not like any of my expectations. In the midst of everything that I was going through, God asked me if I loved Him with all my heart. Did I belong to Him? Did I give myself completely to Him? As a thirteen-year-old, I said no, with a bit of anger. I told Him to take back the gift of "handwriting." But He was patience with me, even when all I did was blame Him. He did not give up on me. He took me under His wing and taught me the true meaning of being a disciple of Jesus Christ.

My mother and I would pray to God to send someone to teach us about the walk with God, step by step. I would pray to God to send me a close friend to whom I could talk about God. My mother and I kept looking for a teacher or a friend that we could physically see, but God had other plans. The Holy Spirit became my teacher, Jesus became my friend, and heaven became my playground. As a disciple of Jesus Christ, all I needed was God, Holy Spirit, Jesus, and the Bible. He wanted me to have faith in Him, and I learned to walk, step by step, with Him by my side. Without even trying, I ended up loving Him with all my heart, with all my soul, and with all my strength. He is the center of my life.

But what does it really mean to put God first and to love Him with all your heart, soul, and strength? What will our lives look like when we actually follow the command in Deuteronomy 6:5? As believers, we all love God at some level, but we never succeed in loving Him with our entire beings at every moment. We love God in church but forget as soon as we get out of church. We pray in the morning but forget to think about Him again for the rest of the day. We don't mean to deliberately do it. We get caught up in our hectic lives, trying to please others. Sometimes, it's because we are trying to be too "Christian." We get caught up in doing too much community service, helping others, going to church or doing church duties, or making money. I'm not saying is bad to do any of that, but God is above everything else. My mother always said, "No matter what you do, if you do not put God first, then it means nothing to Him." No matter what charity you do or what service you bring to church, if you do not do it with a heart that is filled with God, then it means nothing.

Let's take a look at the life of Jesus to fully understand what it means to be a disciple of Jesus Christ. I looked at how others praised God, and I studied their lives as Christians, but God told me not to look at the lives of others but only at His Son, Jesus.

In Jesus' life, there was never a moment when He did not love God with all of His being. And the only way for us to do what He did is to become completely like Him. Being sinners, however, that is impossible. When God first told me to be the image of Jesus Christ and to let my every action be a reflection of Him, I thought, *how could I become the image of Jesus Christ? How can I carry my own cross and follow Jesus? I can barely handle the gift that You gave me. I can't keep any of my promises to You. I am not strong enough to go through even the little hardships and pain with which you have tested me. How can I go through the pain and hardships Jesus went through?*

But the one thing I learned from God is that He can make the impossible possible. Second Corinthians 5:17–21 says that He has exchanged our sinfulness for His righteousness on the cross, making us His new creation. Our only hope to succeed in putting God first is to begin by trusting fully in His promise to cover our sinfulness with His righteous life. Jesus' life was perfect with regard to putting God first. God taught me to look at the way He lived His life and to imitate Him. First John 2:6 tells us to "walk in the manner that He walked," but that is easier said than done. Jesus life was characterized by submission to the Father's will, service to others, and prayer. Notice that first on the list is submission to the Father's will. That's because He put God first, as we should also.

Jesus never pursued worldly ambition in any way and never pursued the glory of this world. I've seen so many pastors who started their walk with God but who were blinded by materialism, status, fame, and money. They looked for the approval of others instead of God. Jesus had every gift, talent, and ability to make Him the most famous and wealthiest man who ever lived, but there was only one goal that He considered worthy of His talents—the glory of the Father.

When I visited heaven, Jesus asked me what I wanted the most in the world. I looked at Him, held His hand, and said, "*You.*" I simply wanted Him. I didn't want Him because

He brought me to heaven. I didn't want Him because He was handsome. I didn't want Him because of His richness or because He could give me all the materialistic things in the world. I simply love Him because I know of His glory, His kindness, and His love that radiates within Him. I gave my life to Him the moment I met Him on my first visit to heaven. I promised myself that the time, resources, energy, gifts, and knowledge of God that I'd been given would not be used to gain influence, make money, or fuel pride but instead to bring glory to His name (Matthew 25:14-30) and to bring the lost souls home (2 Corinthians 5:20), as I trusted God to protect me and provide for me (Matthew 6:31-33). Jesus' life was a perfect picture of loving God with heart, soul, and strength and putting Him first.

In the beginning, I thought that putting God first meant going to church regularly, pleasing people, giving a tithe to any pastors or evangelists, donating regularly, and dressing well to impress others. I thought about my physical appearance and earthly things, but none of this was what the Lord wanted. In the Bible, Jesus never expresses His love for God by singing praises to God or dancing for joy. I'm not saying that Jesus was not joyful; He *was* joyful. Joy is the fruit of the Spirit. Joy can be expressed in many ways. Just as how God give each of us different gifts; teachers, prophets, dreamers, healers, prayers, and etc. We all have our own personal relationship with God. Jesus knew that His actions on earth would bring great joy to God and the joy of the people. Hebrews 12:2 tell us that "Jesus went to the cross with anticipated great joy and was even motivated by it." But isn't that hard to believe?

After all, the snapshot of Jesus' life that we see in the Bible—which I assume God wants us to see and imitate (1 Peter 2:21)—is not really a picture of freedom, happiness, songs, and laughter. In fact, it seems that Jesus' love for God was played out most often in hardship, tears, sorrows, trials, and eventually a painful and horrific death.

I have learned that walking with God and loving Him with all my heart, all my soul, and all my strength is not an easy path (Luke 13:24). In the beginning, people didn't want to do anything with my family and me. Some churches where we were invited to give testimony did not accept the gift that God gave me. There were some people that would come directly to our home and would tell me that they would pray the Devil away. Others would call me a robot and say the Devil created me to give false messages. There were years when I had no friends and no one to talk to. Those weren't my saddest years, though, because the Lord sent three thousand angels to accompany me. After that, there was never a day when I was lonely or depressed. The Lord had given me a peaceful heart. The life of a Christian is a life of joy, despite the trials, and a life that anticipates great joy (2 Corinthians 7:4; Revelation 22:16-17)

Whenever I feel that I can no longer go on with the hardship and pain, I think about Jesus and the hardship He went through because of my sins. Whenever I feel as If I am giving into temptation, I pray and ask God to help me. Whenever I feel as if I'll get lost, I ask God to hold my hand. I know God goes wherever I go (Joshua 1:9). I know that whatever trials and hardships wait for me, God already has won against them all (2 Chronicles 20:17). I do not expect my life to be easy or successful or fulfilling in worldly sense. I don't mind if the world hates me because I stand firm with God. The world isn't my home. I do not belong to the world. I belong to my heavenly Father (John 15:18-19).

A friend once asked me why I would rather read the Bible and pray at home instead of going out and doing fun things with friends. My answer was that even though the world tells us to be someone, to achieve, and to live the good life - after all, you only get to live once they would say but all is a lie. It only brings pain and disappointment (1 Timothy 6:9-10). Nothing can give eternal happiness except God.

Living the life of Jesus is not an easy task. There are days when I still have a hard time living in the command of God. I have a hard time trusting and opening up; I'm an introvert. And I'm still learning every day. There are times when God does get angry with me, when I get stubborn and not listen to His voice, but I know it is because He love me. After all, He knows me better than I know myself. The life of a Christian should be characterized by moment-by-moment selfless service to God, which flows from love for Him. Every day, I want to do better. I want to get to know Him even more. It is never boring to be with Him. There is so much to know about Him, and the more I know Him, the more in love with Him I am. That is what it means to put God first.

If any wealth comes my way, I will use it to generously give. Any success or influence or talents that I might have will be used to multiply God's influence, and any strength or health I enjoy will be spent in His service. My life is His, and everything I am is His. There is nothing in life I want more than Him.

Let's stop trying to be cool

There is one struggle that's been following me for the past five years and that is finding a church. My standard of what kind of church I want isn't high. I simply want a church that focus on God, that addresses important issues of faith even the hard ones, accept the Holy Spirit and simplicity. Churches nowadays focuses too much on being "cool." The goal of church, worship and singing praises to God is to be God-centered, not me-focused. This goes for whole Sunday service, including preaching. You see, we come to church to listen and learn more about God. We're not coming in church to catch up with friends or have some private experience with God. Pastors represent Christ to us. Churches represent Christ. Pastors represent Christ. We represent Christ. But the God that we love is special; He is just not another person. He is the King of Kings and Lord of Lords. Do we no longer have respect for Him?

I loved God. I struggled with loving His church. Many churches focus on the details, trying to follow the trends in social media, music and fashion. When I go to church and listen to service, 90% of the time pastors gossips more than tell the good news of the Lord. Ministers would preach longer about their personal lives, blessings and achievements. I want to learn more about a loving and holy God, not about things on earth. I don't want "cool," I simply want God.

Fear of the Lord

It is important to love the Lord with all your heart, but it is also important to walk in the fear of the Lord. This means to fear, to respect, and to reverence the Lord. It is important to walk in the words of the Lord and to live with wisdom, knowledge, and understanding; as otherwise, you cannot find the real meaning behind fear of the Lord.

> *"Tune your ears to wisdom, and concentrate on understanding.*
> *Cry out for insight, and ask for understanding.*
> *Search for them as you would for silver; seek them like hidden treasures.*
> *Then you will understand what it means to fear the Lord, and you will gain knowledge of God."* - Proverbs 2:2-5

Why is it so important to fear the Lord? Take my oldest brother as an example. If you asked him to choose between God and our mother, he'd choose my mother. And you might think he really loves our mom, but he has no respect for her words. He refuses to listen to her or even spend time with her. He does not respect her decisions. In fact, he has no respect for her and does not fear her at all.

We can proclaim to the world that we love God, but if we do not walk with Him, our words mean nothing to God. If we do not fear God then we refuse to follow His command and His words. It is true that God is the God of love and forgiveness, but God is also the God of anger. You might love reading the Bible verses about God's love, but you also must read the Bible verses about His anger. I see the life of many believers who love God but do not fear Him. They would live a life of non-believers, saying that's what God would want for me. Many believers choose to put earthly things above God. The main cause of these problems is that they do not fear God. So what does walking in fear of God looks like? Deuteronomy 10:12,20-21 explain to us what it means to walk in fear of God, "And now, Israel, what does the Lord your God ask of you but to fear the Lord your God, to walk in obedience to him, to love him, to serve the LORD your God with all your heart and with all your soul ... Fear the Lord your God and serve Him. Hold fast to Him and take your oaths in His name. He is your praise; He is your God, who performed for you those great and awesome wonders you saw with your one eyes." But how important is the fear of God?

Hebrews 12:28-29 explains that we should "worship God acceptably with reverence and awe, for our God is consuming fire." *Proverbs 22:4* states that "*by humility and the fear of the Lord are riches, and honor, and life.*" The rewards for fearing the Lord are strength to turn away from evil, knowledge, wisdom, the basis for contentment, the instruction of wisdom, God's salvation, a satisfying life and strong confidence and refuge. But to obtain these rewards, you would need to know the right type of fear.

There are two types of fear, and to have the right type of fear, we must have wisdom. The right type of fear includes the fear of consequences of disobedience. There might be times when temptation or trials come that we may forget some of the better reasons to obey God, but this is when we have to think of the consequences. *Hebrews 10:26-31* says, "*If we deliberately keep on sinning after we have received the knowledge of the truth, no sacrifice for sins is left, but only a fearful expectation of judgment and of raging fire that will consume the enemies of God. Anyone who rejected the Law of Moses died without mercy on the testimony of two or three witnesses. How much more severely do you think someone deserves to be punished who has trampled the Son of God underfoot, who has insulted the Spirit of grace? For we know him who said, 'it is mine to avenge; I will repay' and again, 'The Lord will judge his people.' It is a dreadful thing to fall into the hands of the living God.*"

The fear of the God is the basis for our walking in His ways, serving Him, and loving Him. But there is also wrong fear of God—a terrifying and paralyzing fear. One example of fear gone wrong is Matthew 25:25. "So I was afraid and went out and hid your gold in the ground. See, here is what belongs to you." That is not the type of fear that God wants us to have

"Cowards, unbelievers, the corrupt, murderers, the immoral, those who practice witchcraft, idol worshipers, and all liars—their fate is in the fiery lake of burning sulfur. This is the second death" (Revelation 21:8).

Cowards will not be in God's kingdom. This fear is not something God is looking for. In the beginning of my walk with God, I misinterpreted His words and His love. My mother and I fear the Lord, but we feared Him the wrong way. We were scared to give our testimony or stand on stage because we thought we weren't worthy to stand in front of godly people. We hid at home for a long time, scared that people would judge us and afraid that we would bring shame to God's name. We thought that if we hid ourselves, the gift that God had given us would never go away and that our faith would never go away. By doing that, however, we weren't growing spiritually, and we weren't doing the job that God gave us to do. So instead of feeling the peace, love, and joy as we first did, we felt lonely, sad, and thirsty for growth. We weren't getting anywhere.

When you know God, you know that there is never such a thing as enough. "The fear of God is an attitude of respect, a response of reverence and wonder. It is the only appropriate response to our Creator and Redeemer" (Nelson's NKJV Study Bible, 1997). The healthy fear of God includes the fear of disobedience. There might be time during temptation or trials when we might forget the reasons for obeying God, and that is the time when we have to remember to think of consequences. "Moses said to the people, 'Do not be afraid. God has come to test you, so that the fear of God will be with you to keep you from sinning'" (Exodus 20:20).

Some of my friends thought that following Jesus Christ and obeying Him was the most depressing thing. They thought that I must lead a very dull life. I told them that when you put God first, when you have a relationship with God, there is never such a thing as a dull moment. I don't need short-term happiness; I don't need earthly entertainment or material things, because the truth is that eternal happiness belongs with God. When I obey Him, I don't obey Him out of fear or because I feel threatened. I obey Him because I love Him.

Once we know God's love, we can never run away from it. I also know that while earthly things are fun for now, they will not last. We are only passing through this earth—we live here only for a hundred or so years, if we get to live for that long.

> If we deliberately keep on sinning after we have received the knowledge of the truth, no sacrifice for sins is left, but only a fearful expectation of judgment and of raging fire that will consume the enemies of God. Anyone who rejected the Law of Moses died without mercy on the testimony of two or three witnesses. How much more severely do you think someone deserves to be punished who has trampled the Son of God underfoot, who has treated as an unholy thing the blood of the covenant that sanctified them, and who has insulted the Spirit of grace? For we know him who said, "It is mine to avenge; I will repay, "and again, "The Lord will judge his people." It is a dreadful thing to fall into the hands of the living God. (Hebrews 10:26–31)

Reverence of God helps us to take Him and His laws seriously. Many of these benefits come in this life, but the greatest benefits will be experienced in the life to come (1 Timothy 4:8). I promised the Lord that my remaining years on earth would be in service to Him. I want to do the best I can for Him so that when judgment day comes, I won't have to worry about things I haven't done. At eighteen years old, I don't worry about boys, going to the club, or pleasing others. Rather, I worry about whether or not I am making my heavenly Father proud. How will I be part of the rapture? What should I improve to have a Christ like image? What should I do to bring people closer to our heavenly Father? These are questions I think about every day.

When Jesus lives inside you, you know from the bottom of your heart what you need to change and what you need to improve. You listen to God—it's as simple as that. There is so much joy in listening to God, obeying Him, and having a relationship with Him.

Obedience

*"Now, if you obey me fully and keep my covenant,
then out of all the nations you will be my treasured
possession. Although the whole earth is mine." -
Exodus 19:5*

One of the most important parts of your relationship with
God is obedience. I learned that at the age of sixteen, and I
am still learning. There are times when I still have a difficult
time obeying God, mainly because I don't quite understand
the plans He has for me or because I have plans of my own.
When I look at the people around me, I do feel discourage
at times. It feels as if everyone is slowly climbing the ladder
of "stable" living situation while my family and I are slowing
going down. There were times when I felt that it was not fair
of God to place us in this situation even though I have been
so faithful and obedient. I would then wonder what my life
would be like if I was not given the gift or was anointed
by the Holy Spirit? Would my life have been better? Then
I remember His love, His kindness, His faithfulness and
His patience. Although we are not rich, we are not poor

either. My heavenly Father has given me a home to stay, a bed to sleep, food to eat and most of all He has shower me with love. Is not a lot but it is "a enough." And despite my many mistakes and foolishness, He has been patiently guiding me close to Him. I have nothing to complain about. My obedience to God has taught me more than I would ever learn as a non-believer. My obedience to God helps me become closer to God and has given me much more happiness than this world could ever give me.

Obedience to God proves our love for Him, demonstrates our faithfulness to Him, and glorifies Him, and opens many blessing for us. But to fully obey and live a life that pleases Him, we must have faith. Obedience comes from faith. *Hebrews 11:8* says, *"By faith Abraham, when called to go to a place he would later receive as his inheritance, obeyed and went, even though he did not know where he was going."* By **faith** Abraham obeyed. The obedience we are talking about right now is not the obedience of a slave but rather the obedience of a child; the obedience of love, not terror; the obedience of faith, not of fear. Have faith in God, and then obey, obey, obey until the Lord call us home. Obey on earth with a genuine and true faith, and then we will live a lifestyle that is pleasing to God. For me, I obey His commands, not because I have to but because I want to, because I love and respect Him. We should not be the same people we once were, because we believe in Christ and are saved. We are remade. Second Corinthians 5:17 says, "If anyone is in Christ, he is a new creation; the old has gone, the new has *come!"*

When we obey our heavenly Father, we live a life of joy, without shame, rooted deeply in the Lord, and confident in our eternal hope. My obedience in God means I truly do have faith in Him and assurance that I truly do know God.

"Blessed are all who fear the Lord, who walk in obedience to Him" (Psalm 128:1).

The Bible tells us that God blesses and rewards obedience.

"Do not merely listen to the word, and so deceive yourselves. Do what it says. Anyone who listens to the word but does not do what it says is like someone who looks at his face in a mirror and, after looking at himself, goes away and immediately forgets what he looks like. But whoever looks intently into the perfect law that gives freedom, and continues in it—not forgetting what they have heard, but doing it—they will be blessed in what they do" (James 1:22–25).

But sometimes as Christians, even though we do know that obedience is important, it's difficult to stay on the correct path every single day. And that is why we should do things to strengthen our obedience and not weaken it. We should not expose ourselves to unhealthy temptations. I've seen many who say they can't stop drinking, yet they keep buying alcohol. So to strengthen obedience, we should focus on the positive aspects in our lives, meditate on Bible verses, and pray, asking God to guide us.

Purity

"Blessed are the pure in heart, for they will see God." —Matthew 5:8

You might think the title of this chapter refers to sexual purity, but I'll be talking about purity in heart. Sexual purity is also important; many have talked about it but very few people talk about purity in heart. The Greek word for "pure" in Matthew 5:8 is *katharous*. It means to be "clean, blameless, unstained from guilt." The word can refer specifically to that which is purified by fire or by pruning. John the Baptist told people that Jesus would baptize with the Holy Spirit and fire (Matthew 3:11). Malachi speaks of the Messiah as being like a "refiner's fire" (Malachi 3:2). Jesus refers to believers as being the branches and to Himself as being the vine (John 15:1-17).

I learned that for a vine to produce fruit, it must be pruned. Those who are truly "pure" are those who have been declared innocent because of the work of Jesus and who are sanctified by His refining fire and His pruning. So who is pure of heart? Only those who fully surrendered their own heart completely to Jesus and are unstained by their own evil desires.

I've seen people who turn away from God because they felt pressured, confused, angry and broken. They love their earthly live more then God. Those people are people who attempt to live a double life spiritually - pure on the outside when they are not pure in heart. They are restless, wretched, confused, and tense. They cannot find peace in their heart. They can't quite decide on which lives they want.

I know someone who loves God but is afraid to die. She said she'd much rather live in this world. The material things on earth appalled her. Her eyes are on two matters at once, and her vision is blurred so that neither image is clear.

An article compiled by Richard A.Kauffman says, "Opposing purity of heart is lust of any kind—money, vengeance, and sexual access to others—whether indulged through actions or imaginations. A pure heart will loves God with the whole heart and soul and mind." Whenever I pray, I never forget to tell God that I love Him with all my heart, soul, and mind. He has no rival and is worthy of our adoration and praise. You are the only one. I strive to see God. I am always on fire with the desire of seeing God, to always be in His presence. The pure hearts are blessed because they will see God.

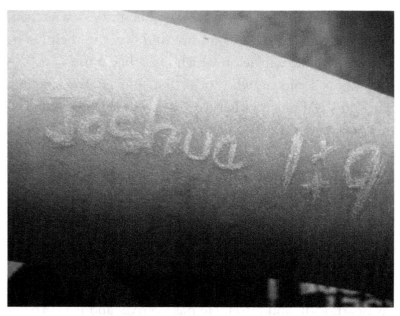

"This is my command – be strong and courageous! Do not be afraid or discouraged. For the Lord your God is with you wherever you go." – Joshua 1:9

(2.21.12)

"Don't worry about anything; instead, pray about everything. Tell God what you need, and thank him for all that he has done. Then you will experience God's peace, which exceeds anything we can understand. His peace will guard your hearts and minds as you live in Christ Jesus." – Philippians 4:6-7

(1.7.2010, 12.16.2010, 3.13.11)

"You adulterers! Don't you realize that friendship with the world makes you an enemy of God? I say it again: if you want to be a friend of the world, you make yourself an enemy of God." - James 4:4

(3.10.2011, 7.21.2010)

"This includes you who were once far away from God. You were his enemies, separated from him by your evil thoughts and actions. ²² Yet now he has reconciled you to himself through the death of Christ in his physical body. As a result, he has brought you into his own presence, and you are holy and blameless as you stand before him without a single fault." – Colossians 1:21-22

(1.6.2010)

"And there will be strange signs in the sun, moon, and stars. And here on earth the nations will be in turmoil, perplexed by the roaring seas and strange tides. People will be terrified at what they see coming upon the earth, for the powers in the heavens will be shaken. Then everyone will see the Son of Man coming on a cloud with power and great glory. So when all these things begin to happen, stand and look up, for your salvation is near!" – Luke 21:25-28 (12.26.10)

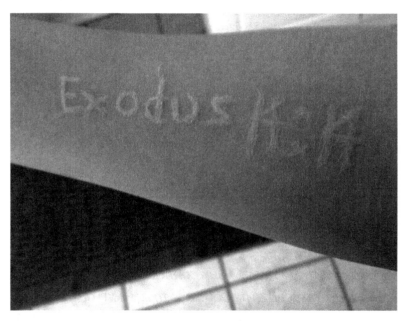

"The Lord himself will fight for you. Just stay calm" –
Exodus 14:14

"*So do not throw away your confidence; it will be richly rewarded. You need to persevere so that when you have done that will of God, you will receive what he has promised. For, 'In just a little while, he who is coming will come and will not delay.' And, 'my righteousness one will live by faith. And I take no pleasure in the one who shrinks back.'*"
– Hebrews 10:35-38

Faith

"For we live by faith, not by sight."
—2 Corinthians 5:7

My faith in God means that I rely on Him and depend on His reliability. Having faith means that I realize that God is bigger, greater, and better than I am—and He loves me greatly. In the past six years, I've had to learn to give myself completely to Him. I've had to learn to trust Him and to stop taking control of the situations. My faith in Him has opened up so much knowledge of Him and has kept me going when all things seem to fail me.

As a new Christian at age thirteen, I thought that being a disciple of God meant I would receive many blessings and have forever happiness. I thought it meant there would be no more hardship or pain. My definition of blessings and happiness at the time was lots of money, a big house, expensive clothing, and expensive cars—the media influenced this and what other people thought was important. I used to think that if I was taller, prettier, or from a well-off family, then I would be happy. I thought that as soon as I accepted Jesus Christ in my life, all the riches in the world would be mine.

Many preachers I heard at the time spoke of the many blessings in their lives, yet none talked about the hardship and trials they had to go through. Some would preach about accepting Jesus Christ, yet none taught us about the journey to walking with God. For the first few years of my walk with God, I was lost. I was foolish and had no wisdom or knowledge. I didn't even know how to begin praying. I had no one to tell me that nothing is impossible with God. There were times when I thought that everybody's idea of what was right was true. I followed what they thought was right but ended up in the wrong.

"There is a path before each person that seems right, but it ends in death" (Proverbs 14:12).

My mother and I refuse to think about the about the first few years of my walk with God. Whenever we think back to those years, we realize how foolish and stupid we were. The first mistake we made as disciples of Jesus Christ was that we forgot to ask what He wanted. We forgot to listen to His voice and instead, we listened to our own earthly interests and to the voices of others—voices of doubters, skeptics, cynics, and nonbelievers. I allowed them to make the choices in my life, and I walked where they wanted me to walk. I remember people calling me "Satan follower," a robot, and mentally ill. I knew from the bottom of my heart that it wasn't true, but I had let the voices of others get to me to the point that I refused to believe that God used me as well.

I questioned God and didn't rely on Him. I had chosen to rely on the people around me. That was my second mistake as a Christian and as the daughter of Jesus Christ. What I thought was right at the time was wrong to God. What I thought was the best plan for my life was not the plan that God had built for me. I couldn't understand why everything I did at the time never went the way I planned. I was not giving myself completely to Him. I did not put Him first above everything else in my life.

Only after two years did I finally pull myself away from others. I finally sat down and asked God to guide me, step by step. I had to put my faith in Him and rely on God's direction. The way God used me might not make sense to others, but it was God's way of getting His message through to others.

Because I am gifted in a way that makes no sense at all, I had to have faith, to keep walking to the finish line and move forward to the purpose He had planned for me. Hebrews 11:6 tell us that without faith, it is impossible to please God, so our relationship with our heavenly Father is dependent on it. Faith is what brings the things God has provided for us from the spiritual realm into the physical realm (Hebrews 11: 1).

I had no spiritual wisdom or knowledge in the early years of my walk with God, because I was not listening to His voice. Whenever He said, "Trust me," I didn't. Whenever He said, "Lean on me," I didn't. He kept knocking, and when I still did not open the door, He blew the door away.

Faith is so important to me during my walk with God, but it did not come naturally to me. There was a lot of anger, pain, and crying. John 3:30 say, "He must become greater; I must become less." I don't know how many times I promised myself that I would wait on God, but I was dying to take control of the situation. I was very impatient and very young. God had to teach me step by step.

Faith is the victory that enables us to overcome the world. Everything the Lord does for us is accessed through faith. I didn't know how to use my faith in the beginning. I didn't even know what faith was until three years after I was given the gift of the writing. Faith is like having a brand new Apple or Galaxy product and knowing its potential but not having a clue how to use it. When I got my first Apple laptop, it came with a detailed instruction manual, but I was too impatient to read through it. My impatient to read through the detailed instruction made me not understand how the laptop functions work. When I decided to randomly browse through the functions, my laptop begins to have many problems and kept shutting down randomly. The Bible is our own detailed instruction manual, but few people take the time to really study it. We are too impatient and choose to go through life with our own instruction. We might reach some level of success, but to really be proficient in life and in our walk with God, we need to read the Bible, take time to pray, and ask the Holy Spirit to explain what each verse is trying to teach. We have to put faith in God's grace, but the faith that we have to use isn't our own human faith. We have to use the faith that is the gift of God.

Human faith can only believe in something that is within human reach—what we can see, taste, hear, smell, or feel. For example, using human faith, we can sit in a chair we've never sat in and believe it will hold us up. When I flew to Dallas, I trusted the pilot, who was a stranger to me, to land the airplane safely at my destination. That takes human faith, which God gives to everyone. But would you sit in a chair you can't see? When it comes to God, we have to believe in things that we cannot see, but how do we do this? The answer is that we can't believe in invisible things with human faith. We need God's supernatural faith.

When everyone around me called me "Satan's child," I had to rely on my faith and my love for God to keep me sane and to let God lead me to His sole purpose. I am limited, but my God is not. God calls things that are not as though they are. An article by Andrew Wommack says, "When we hear God's Word, the Holy Spirit empowers it, and if we receive the truth, God's supernatural faith enters us. We were so destitute that we couldn't even believe the good news on our own. God had to make his kind of faith available to us so that we could believe in Him and receive His salvation. We were saved by using God's supernatural faith to receive His grace."

The more you know about faith and how it works, the better faith will work for you. God is pushing you to move forward; He wants you to move forward. Of course, God loves you just the way you are, but He loves you too much to leave you that way. Now, this doesn't mean we should fixate on a future version of who we think God wants us to be. Instead, we have to learn to be still and know that God is God (Psalm 46:10) and to intimately know that we love, because God first loved us (1 John 4:19).

When I was fifteen years old, I was desperate to become better for God. I knew God loved me, but I wanted to please Him. So instead of asking God to help me become a better disciple of Jesus Christ, I took matters into my own hands and tried to change. It didn't go so well. I ended up trying to be someone that I was not. I begin to hate myself, because I wasn't becoming the change I wanted to be. The truth is, though, that I didn't need to work hard to change. All I had to do was ask God to help me transform. I had to first understand the unconditional love that God has for me. I had to allow myself to *just be* without the emphasis on the need for growth. I had to understand that there is nothing that I can do to make God love me any more or any less and that I didn't need to change anything to be a recipient of that love. As I begin to understand that, I allowed myself to become consumed with His love. As American author and priest Brennan Manning once stated, "Only when God's love for us goes from information in our head to a deep understanding in our heart, does lasting transformation come about." In the past six years of my walk with God, I have learned that Christianity is not about trying harder to be a good person. I learn that is about recognizing and becoming empowered by the gift of the Holy Spirit, beauty, and passion, in the person Jesus, which leads me in gratitude to seek to match. Once we understand His love, learn to put our faith in God, and begin to completely give in to the anointed power of the Holy Spirit, everything will make sense. We will understand and begin to know Him. As our understanding of God's love for us as we are increases, so will our gratitude and our desire to live gladly in the life of the beloved into which God has called us. There is so much to learn about Him. Our souls thirst for Him, and only when we meet Him will our thirst end.

Blessing or Curse

"Brother will betray brother to death, and a father his child; and children will rise up against parents and cause them to be put to death. "You will be hated by all because of my name, but it is the one who has endured to the end who will be saved."— Matthew 10:21-22

When I was first gifted with the handwriting and was saved, I had expectations. As I've mentioned, I thought that being a Christian meant life would be perfect on earth— no hardships, no pain, no financial problems—filled with rainbows and unicorns. Expectations help preface either disappointment or fulfillment. Unfortunately for me, the reality of being a Christian was a shocking letdown, compared to what some pastors, churches, and other believers preach. As I've mentioned, few pastors preached about the great blessing in heaven or what it really means to follow Jesus Christ.

When I was thirteen and given a gift that no one would believe, I questioned who I was as a person and what it meant to walk with God. I'd previously thought that to be a Christian, I had to be perfect. But when my walk with God started, everything He taught me was different from what I'd learned from the people I knew. God's gift to me was so powerful—so beyond human ability—that people would say, "Your gift must be from Satan!" Friends drifted away from me, and the people we had called our close family friends had nothing but bad things to say about my family and me. I was confused, as the things I experienced were nothing like what I imagined. Everywhere I went I stuck out like a sore thumb. People would question me, asking me to make the handwriting come out right in front of them. The number-one reason why people had a hard time believing that God had given me this gift was because I was "unsuitable." But God has a track record of choosing the most unsuitable people in society to accomplish His will.

I come from a family of six; we weren't rich, but we weren't poor. We don't have the best status in my community, but we don't have the worst either. Because we were somewhere in the middle in that regard, people had a hard time putting us in the same room as God. They didn't realize that God does not judge based on our appearance, our status, our worth, or our mistakes. He judges us based on our hearts.

I am not saying I had the purest heart, but I was as pure as a thirteen-year-old would be. I never had bad intentions and never questioned God. I was probably too trusting and very naive. The first two years of my walk with God were probably the worst years of my life. Even now, I can't talk about it without breaking down in tears.

I want to explain a little more about the handwriting on my arms. It wasn't just "on" my arms. Each letter would come out from the inside of my skin—very much like writing looks or feels with a notary seal embosser. Have you ever felt the letters after a paper is stamped with a seal embosser? That's how the handwriting on my arms felt, and feeling the handwriting was probably my favorite thing.

In total, there were over nine hundred handwritings on my arms, most of them Bible verses. Some of the messages that weren't Bible verses are sentences such as "I am coming soon," "I am God," "Don't be afraid," "Peace and joy," and "I am the beginning and the end." Each one of the handwritings was a special message. Some were encouragements, some were warnings, some were teachings, and some were about the love that God has for us.

Let's go back to the many hardships and trials that we have to go through as Christians. Don't get me wrong—following Christ is beautiful and worthwhile, but disappointment, pain, suffering, betrayal, and hurt are also part of life, and Christians aren't immune to or excluded from those horrors. Following Jesus Christ demands sacrifice, honesty, vulnerability, and conflict. It's a commitment that cannot be taken lightly.

When the handwriting started, my mother and I didn't show it to anyone except the prayer group, in which there were about five people. My mother and I knew that the handwriting was a gift that others would have a hard time believing. Even from the beginning, we worried more about what others would say than what God had to say. The plans that we thought were perfect were not the plans that God had for us.

One night, while the prayer group and I were praying in the basement of my aunt's house, the words of Mark 16:15 appeared on my arm: "Go into all the world and preach the gospel to all creation."

God already had a plan for me, and the Lord's purposes will prevail. Proverbs 21:30 say, "There is no wisdom, no insight, no plan that can succeed against the LORD." In the beginning, whenever we saw a Bible verse, we thought we had to go door-to-door and explain about the gift that God had given me. We thought we should go from church to church and show the handwriting to the people, but that was not God's plan.

Regardless of the plans we make as wise or insightful people, nothing will overcome the purposes and plans of the Lord. While my mother and I worried how to spread the gospel, God had already spread it around. Somehow, people knew about the handwriting, and people from across the world begin to call and visit, asking to see the handwriting and wanting me to tell them the whole story on how the handwriting started.

But when we are called to serve the Lord, that privilege comes with both blessings and hardships. Anointment invites trials and suffering, but do not worry. We have the full armor of God—His truth, His righteousness, His Word, and our salvation, which He gives, not because we earn it but because He loves us.

When people began to take an interest in the miracle with which God had gifted me, so did the Enemy. When people visited our house, some had good intentions, but others came with bad intentions. I felt as if my every move was being watched, as if someone was hoping to catch some kind of mistake. I didn't quite understand how people could turn so quickly against me. People who I thought were my friends would tell me to stop doing whatever I was doing. I was confused—how could I stop doing it when I didn't even know what I was doing wrong. Old friends visited me at home, saying they would "pray the Devil" out of me. A pastor told me that I should not go out, in order to stop further embarrassment.

Whenever I would sit in my living room, my father would come in and ask me to get mental checkup. My father's side of the family would call every day, asking me to see a doctor to find out if was going crazy. Some people thought I did the handwriting myself. I was trusting and naïve, and I couldn't understand why people would call me "mental" or "Satan's child." There was nothing I could do to stop the handwriting—or to create it. It is not within human ability to have nine hundred bible verses come out of your skin.

There were moments in the beginning when I thought God must really hate me to give me such a gift. I would pray to God, asking for the gift of singing, or prophecy, or healing. For a few years, I thought my gift was a curse rather than blessing. As friends drifted away and people continued to gossip about me, I felt as if I was watching a nightmare played in front of me. When I gave myself completely to God, I did not ask for the gift of handwriting, nor did I ask for my life to turn out this way.

I didn't think that being a follower of Jesus Christ would be this difficult. I was being pulled left and right, being dragged to places I did not wish to go, and getting criticized in everything I did, simply because of my gift, Still, I wasn't afraid. I felt peace and joy in my heart. Romans 15:13 says, "Now may the God of hope fill you with all joy and peace in believing, so that you will abound in hope by the power of the Holy Spirit."

Every fiber in my body told me the gift was from God, and I was desperate for His presence and the fire inside of me. I wanted others to feel what I felt. I wanted them to feel the love, joy, and peace that consumed me. Of course, I was angry with God for making me go through this pain and hardship, but at the same time, I loved Him with all my heart. I wanted to please Him. I wanted others to see what I saw. I wanted others to feel what I was feeling. But no one understood.

When people would visit me at home, I prayed that God would show them the handwriting, but sometimes it came and sometimes it didn't. When it did come, however, they still wouldn't believe it. I later felt that it was a waste of time, as they still refused to see that the handwriting was from God. When it didn't come, they would call me a liar, a mental child.

There were times when I hated the handwriting so much that I asked my mother to just cut off my arms—I didn't want them. My mother would yell at me and tell me to be thankful for the gift that God had given me.

Now, when I think back to those days, I realize how foolish I was. I expected things to get better for me. I assumed God would shine down His divine blessings—salary increases, social popularity, better grades in school, and maybe even a bigger house. I wanted my faith to work for me, not the other way around. Whenever I met people, the questions they all asked were often similar:

Did you write the handwriting on your arms by yourself?

It was not possible for me to write more than nine hundred messages on my skin by myself—and without any scars. Sometime six or seven handwritings came on my arms in a day; sometimes the handwriting would change in two or three seconds. That is beyond human ability. Also, at the age of thirteen – fourteen years old, I had only started reading Genesis. I did not know any of the bible chapters or bible verses.

Is the handwriting from Satan? How can you be sure you're not being used by the Devil?

The handwriting was mostly Bible verses and praises to God. Lots of them were to bring glory to God's name. My heart longed for God, and I was desperate for His love, His presence, and His words. There was nothing in me that was wrong. I was simply consumed by His love. I could talk about God forever. How could I be from the Devil when I have so much love for Jesus? I can't understand why we put so many limits on the things God can do, yet we don't put limits on the Devil. Have people forgotten that our God is the most powerful God? Nothing is impossible for God.

A pastor from another state visited me at home. When he asked me if I'd written the handwriting by myself, I told him that there was no reason for me to write the handwriting—after all, I wasn't getting any money, fame, or positive attention from it. All I got was negative attention and getting called ugly names. I had no friends, and people looked at me like I was an alien from another planet. No one knew how painful it was for me to be the center of negative attention at thirteen years old. There were nights when I couldn't sleep and would ask God to take back the gift because I couldn't handle the burden, hardship, and pain that came with it. But sometimes God gives us more than we can handle, not because He wants us to suffer but because He is with us. And because He is with us, there is no such thing as "can't."

He Does Give You More than You Can Handle

"No temptation has overtaken you except what is common to mankind. And God is faithful; he will not let you be tempted beyond what you can bear. But when you are tempted, he will also provide a way out so that you can endure It." —1 Corinthians 10:13

I don't know how many times I cried to God and said the words "I can't," yet I would keep going. The truth is, God never said He wouldn't give you more than you can handle. He will give you more then you can handle, but He will be with you every step of the way. There were times in life when I felt like I was drowning, and there was no one to help me. There were times when I felt like screaming or punching someone when they give me words of encouragement or when someone says, "I know what you are going through." When I was down and discouraged, hearing words of encouragement often felt like someone is stepping on me.

It felt as if people were ignoring my suffering and pretending as if it wasn't there. Then there were times when I would look in the mirror and lie to myself, telling myself that I could do it, that things will get better and that is okay if no one in this world understand what I am going through. I kept feeling sorry for myself but through all that suffering and digging a hole for myself, I forgot to do one thing—and that was to call on God.

Many times we try to handle hardships and pain on our own, and when things don't work out, we blame God. But that's not why God gives us these trials and temptations. God wants us to realize that we can't make it on our own. I'll bet that while I was going crazy and feeling sorry for myself in my room, God was standing right next to me, waiting for me to ask Him for help. He wants us to ask Him for help. Paul warns us about the reality of temptation and sin that meet us every day. But with his warning, he had also given us a promise. It took me a while to really understand the meaning behind 1 Corinthians 10:13. "No temptation has overtaken you except what is common to mankind. And God is faithful; he will not let you be tempted beyond what you can bear. But when you are tempted, he will also provide a way out so that you can endure it." Paul is saying that we always have a choice: give in to the temptation of sin or run far away from it. The promise Paul gave is that God will always provide a way for us to not given in to temptation. But let's be clear about one thing: Paul was only talking about temptation, not suffering. With temptation, we have a choice, but with suffering, we have no one to lean on except God.

Rather than proclaiming we can handle it, we should imitate Jesus Christ. In the past six years, I have become aware that life has given me more than I can handle, but I have come to grips with it. During those six years, however, God made a promise to me: He is faithful in meeting me in any temptation, trial, or pain. I've learned to recognize my constant need to depend on Him.

God instructed me to cast my worries, fears, and suffering on to Him. The reason we each can do that is because God cares for us. When our burdens become another's burdens, we become an instrument through which our heavenly Father can bless another. We become the living proof that while the life of a Christian can sometimes be too much, through the goodness and power of our loving God, we can move forward to where He is waiting for us and be the testimony for our mighty God.

Trust

"The LORD will fight for you; you need only to be still." —Exodus 14:14

For a long time, much of the writing on my arms was Bible verses about trust. When I was thirteen, and the people that I thought I could rely on and trust turned their backs on me, I began to have trust issues. My mother and my brothers were the only ones I called a family. As I grew older, I put my new friends at arm's length away from me—I wanted no one to be anywhere near my heart.

If you were to ask me what scares me the most, I would say disobedience toward God, disobedience toward my mom, and getting my heart broken. I am very sensitive, and even if I put on a façade of being a strong and emotionless person, I feel a lot and am hurt easily. The first few years of my walk with God broke my heart to pieces because of the names that people called me when they refused to believe in the gift that God gave me. I felt a need to control my life again, but God did not want that. I often wondered why God made me suffer so much, especially since people's words were like knife. I would have much rather been hurt physically than emotionally. Now, as an eighteen-year-old, I understand why God allowed me to suffer.

I was not leaning toward His strength or Him in the beginning. I was so focused on hating the gift, the hurt, and Him that I could not see the bigger picture. He wanted me to look at Him and no other. I gained wisdom, knowledge, and understanding through each hardship and pain that I went through. He loves me and had given me the freedom to choose. It was not that God allowed me to suffer but that I was too blind to choose Him. I chose to please the people—the friends who had turned their backs on me, the people who did not believe the gift that God had given me. I forgot to look at Him, the one who had given me the gift.

Now I choose Him. Suffering is still there, pain is still there, and the hardship is still there—these are Satan's ways of trying to make me turn against God, but I know the Lord that I am serving. My heavenly Father has won against all my enemies. I trust Him and the road that He is leading me toward. It will not be easy, but I know He is holding my hand and that I am walking with Him. I feel it in my heart—the peace, the love, and the happiness that is overcoming every fiber in my body.

Don't Limit God

"Is anything too hard for the Lord?"
—Genesis 18:14

For the first three years of my walk with God, I asked myself every day, "Is anything too hard for the Lord?" When discouragement, pain, and suffering begin to eat me up, I would remember that my Father is the King of Kings, the Lord of Lords. He created heaven and earth. Nothing is impossible for Him. He has won against all my enemies and fears. Sometimes we might limit God to what human ability can do and to what our human mind can imagine, but I learned that God's ability and power is way beyond what we can imagine. God's power and wisdom are beyond our comprehension.

When people first saw the writing on my arms, a large number of them immediately decided that the handwriting was from Satan. I couldn't understand why they would assume it was from Satan, simply because it was something beyond human ability. God is *huge*! First Kings 8:27 say that even the entire universe can't contain Him. He is infinite.

When the handwriting first appeared, I had no doubts that it was from God. I accepted Jesus Christ in my life, and every fiber of my being was at peace. But when others begin to question the handwriting and criticize my faith in God, I wondered if God really had the ability to give me this gift. Was I really from Him? My heart was saying yes, but my head told me that scientific logic made much more sense. But the Lord spoke to me through dreams and with people God sent in my life.

Each one of us has a gift—they're all different gifts, but each one of us has one. Sadly, life and the Devil do a pretty good job of taking the gifts out of us. The Devil lets us think that we are limited in what we can accomplish. We begin to doubt our God, and day-by-day we forget who God is and how powerful and loving He is. We let the Devil beat us down with discouragement, depression, doubt, and pain. God has plans for each of us that exceed what we are experiencing and that are beyond our imagination. We were created for greatness.

But we should not confuse what the world calls greatness with what God calls greatness—these are two different things. "Every man's work shall be made manifest; for the day shall declare it, because it shall be revealed by fire; and the fire shall try every man's work of what sort it is" (1 Corinthians 3:13). The verse says that every man's work "shall be revealed by the fire" on what sort it is, not what size it is. We are all created by God to influence the world, to make a difference, and to tell the good news to the world. We are created, most importantly, to tell the good news of the Lord. We cannot do that if we limit God due to our disbelief or doubts or because we have a hard time having faith in God.

One of the greatest mistakes we limit to what God can do in our lives is by being inspired by what God is doing in others. We judge people according to their flesh. The main reason why people had a hard time believing that God had anointed me was because I did not have any status, parents of great influence, or wealth. People judged me based on outward things like appearance. In stature and speech, I was not the greatest. I did not come from a well-off family, and I was a little too quiet and shy, but God saw something in me and chose to give me a gift. For years I felt that I was not worthy to be anointed by God. I let what others said get inside my head, which in return limited God. After many attempts from God to break through my hard head, I finally realized that I was limiting God by putting myself down and not having enough faith in Him.

People around me limited God with their greediness, status, money, and materialism. We sometimes forget that we are limited, but God is not. He has the ability to give me the gift of the handwriting to get His message to the world. Our God is a God who created heaven and earth, who raised His one and only Son, Jesus Christ, from death. Our God is the most powerful and almighty and is forever to be praised.

The Kind Of Preaching
God Wants

"They devoted themselves to the apostles' teaching and the fellowship, to the breaking bread and the prayers ... And all who believed were together and had all things in common ... breaking bread in their homes ... praising God and having favor with all people. And the Lord added to their number day by day those who were being saved." - Acts 2:42, 44, 46-47

In the past six years that I've walked with God, I have come to dislike going to church. Don't get me wrong; I didn't give up on God. I love God and still wish to serve Him with every fiber in my being, but I have given up on the people and things that *represent* God. I still listen to the Word of God through evangelical pastors, such as David Jeremiah, Charles Stanley, R. C. Sproul, and Rick Warren. I've tried to find a church that is filled with the Holy Spirit and that puts God first, above everything else, but I have not found one near me. I'm not saying that I need the "perfect" church; my expectations are realistic. I've found, however, that a lot of churches either have hidden racism or the pastor puts people first or money first and criticizes others or other pastors.

I've thought about it, again and again—what are churches these days missing? All the evidence points to one answer: God and the Holy Spirit. I find that churches tend to care more about duties and money and tend to preach about what they think people want to hear. Many people have their own opinions on what kind of preaching they desire, but they forget the real question: what kind of preaching does God want us to preach? I've learned that a lot of Christians say, "I'm sure that's what God wants," or they focus on only one verse from the Bible that they like and forget the other verses.

We live in a time when churches worry more about money, attendance, fashion, music and society than on focusing solely on God. Some people just want to feel good about the message they hear; they don't want to hear anything that needs to change in their lives to be right with God or that our relationship with Christ comes with hardship and pain. I've seen so many preachers start with the Word of God, and then they begin to teach words that others want to hear or the many earthly blessing they receive and gossip about others. This kind of preaching comes as a warning to Timothy from Paul:

> In the presence of God and of Christ Jesus,
> who will judge the living and the dead, and
> in view of his appearing and his kingdom,

I give you this charge: Preach the word; be prepared in season and out of season; correct, rebuke and encourage—with great patience and careful instruction. For the time will come when people will not put up with sound doctrine. Instead, to suit their own desires, they will gather around them a great number of teachers to say what their itching ears want to hear. They will turn their ears away from the truth and turn aside to myths. But you, keep your head in all situations, endure hardship, and do the work of an evangelist, discharge all the duties of your ministry. (1 Timothy 4:1-5)

Sometimes people don't want God's teachings. Instead, to suit their own desires, they want them to preach things that pleases their ears, even If what they preach will lead many down the road to destruction. I once heard a pastor tell the church that it was okay to keep sinning because God would always forgive them. It is true that God will forgive all our sins, but if we keep going back to the sin that we know is wrong in God's eyes, we do not have a relationship with God. As Christians, we need to read our Bibles and find out what God wants preachers to preach and what God wants us to do and change. It doesn't matter how many times we study our Bible, we need to keep studying the words of God. There is so much to discover about Him. This lifetime is not enough to find out about our heavenly Father.

Over the years, I've seen preachers tell stories and briefly mention Scriptures, but that does not mean they are preaching the truth. When preachers do it their way instead of God's way, it causes the congregation to lose respect for God's Word and allows false doctrines to enter in. This is why Paul warns Timothy that if the Word of God is not taught, then people will go astray. Paul tells Timothy many times in his letters that he should keep the Word of God close and teach others to keep the Word of God.

So how does one preach the way God want us to preach? First Timothy 4:6 tell us, "If you point these things out to the brothers and sisters, you will be a good minister of Christ Jesus, nourished on the truths of the faith and of the good teaching that you have followed."

A disciple of Jesus Christ is one who instructs other Christians with the Word of God. When this is done, this will help provide the listeners with what they need to hear and not necessarily what they want to hear. God wants a preacher who will addresses difficult issues, so their hearts will be pricked, and they will realize that they need to repent and change their ways. I've found that this is not something lot of preachers enjoy doing—after all, who really likes being no one's favorite —but if he is preaching the Word of God, filled with the Holy Spirit, and puts God first above everything else, he will preach on topics that will eventually touch everyone. Last year, an evangelist I know came to the United States from Burma. His teachings are a bit hard to understand to those who do not accept the Holy Spirit. His teachings are not things that others want to hear. He addresses difficult issues and teaches things the way it is; he doesn't sugarcoat his words. In the beginning, listeners had a hard time accepting him but as time goes by, they begin to slowly understand and accept his teaching. Even though we all have different weaknesses and strengths, God's Word covers them all. As Peter says, "Grace and peace be yours in abundance through the knowledge of God and of Jesus our Lord. His divine power has given us everything we need for a godly life through our knowledge of him who called us by His own glory and goodness" (2 Peter 1:2).

There were times when people would ask me to ask God if He would be blessing them any time soon or if God was going to give them riches. I would point out that if that was their reason for being a Christian or if that was their way of loving God, then it was not right. I personally don't like pointing out the sins of others or teaching adults, who are older than I am, the way of life with God. But I rejoice, knowing that the words I said, which came from God, led some people to repentance. God want people to understand. His words are very simple and very easy to translate, but people make them difficult. Some preachers like to show off how intelligent they are, and their lessons are filled with difficult terms that most people cannot follow.

I once saw a preacher who began with a great message but ended up losing his message, because he wanted to show off his knowledge of the Bible and his authority in church. Again, that is not the kind of preaching God wants for His people. God wants His preachers to preach His Word plainly with clarity.

God wants a preacher who preaches with humility and out of love for the people and who preaches the truth.

Another thing I learned from God is that He wants a preacher to preach things that please God and not man. For a long time, I was very careful to talk about the things that God opened up to me. I didn't want to offend anyone and didn't want people to hate me or think that I was judging them. I treated God's Word very lightly and instead would listen to the words of others. I spoke, as they wanted me to speak. But God helped me realize that I didn't offend that person; God's Word did.

Paul emphasizes in Galatians 1:6—12 that there is only one doctrine, and we must not teach another, but he also teaches us that God's Word cannot be adjusted to what others want to hear. There are many pastors who rather teach what others want to hear than what God want them to preach.

Whenever I feel a little scared of speaking the Word of God to others, I get encouragement from the following Scripture in Matthew: "What I tell you in the dark, speak in the daylight; what is whispered in your ear, proclaim from the roofs. Do not be afraid of those who kill the body but cannot kill the soul. Rather, be afraid of the One who can destroy both soul and body in hell. Are not two sparrows sold for a penny? Yet not one of them will fall to the ground outside your Father's care" (Matthew 10:27-29).

My goal in life is to be like Jesus' disciples Peter and John, because they took this advice to heart and were arrested for preaching about Jesus. When Jews threatened them, they replied, "Which is right in God's eyes: to listen to you, or to him? You be the judges! As for us, we cannot help speaking about what we have seen and heard" (Acts 4:19-20).

For a long time I was scared of speaking the Word of God. In the beginning, people would criticize me. Some didn't want to listen because I was too young or because of my background. So for the next year or so, I hid away from God. I felt unworthy to be anointed, to be called to preach the good news. Whenever God called for me, I would give Him excuses—I'm too short, too young—but then I looked at the lives of Jesus, Peter, John, and Paul and at their strong faith and love for God. I took strength from their lives and that they simply preached the truth. After all, God will be the judge, not anyone else on earth.

The most important part that I learned from God is that He wants us to live by the Word of God. We cannot preach the Word of God if we do not live by it. First Timothy 4:12 says, "Let no one despise your youth, but be an example to the believers in word, in conduct, in love, in spirit, in faith, in purity." If we do not live our lives according to God's Word, yet we teach the Word, then we are no better than the Pharisees of Jesus' time, or we are like Judas who betrayed Jesus, because of our selfish desires or for putting earthly things above God. We are to be faithful to Him and live our lives with the Word of God.

It's Okay—I'm Forgiven

"What then? Shall we sin because we are not under the law but under grace? By no means! Don't you know that when you offer yourselves to someone as obedient slaves, you are slaves of the one you obey—whether you are slaves to sin, which leads to death, or to obedience, which leads to righteousness?" —Romans 6:15-16

In my earlier years of knowing God, I took advantage of His love and used it however I wanted. I thought, *He loves me and will always forgive me, no matter how many time I repeat my sins.* I wouldn't listen to Him, was not afraid of him, and wouldn't spend more time with Him than I had to. I knew I was not doing the right thing, yet I felt that because He loved me, He would let me off the hook. After all, Jesus already died for my sins. A friend of mine once said: "Is okay to sin. God loves to forgive anyway. What a wonderful arrangement." But Paul confronts such thinking in Romans 6:15-16. I was becoming a slave to sin. I loved Him, but I did not want to follow and obey Jesus Christ. I was more in love with things in the world than with my heavenly Father. It is a serious problem when we take advantage of God's mercy and continue to sin, never repenting or even trying to turn our behavior in God's direction. There is a person who knows the Bible, believe in God and receive Jesus Christ yet continue to sin continually. He'll ask for forgiveness every afternoon after he finishes drinking or smoking yet never wants to repent from his sin. Romans 6:15–16 says we have a choice of what's at the center of our lives: sin or Christ. I knew what I was doing was wrong, but I was too scared to give my life fully to God. I kept saying to myself that God could wait. I could go back at any time, and He would be there waiting, ready to forgive me. I was looking for happiness and love, and I thought that earthly entertainment could give me that satisfaction. I was wrong. I was happy, but it didn't last long.

We try moving our attention to different things, trying to find joy and happiness through different entertainment, yet it never lasts long. When I was done living in the moment, I would go back home, and the loneliness and longing would creep back into my heart. I realized that I was making the wrong choice. I was becoming a slave to sin, an earthly entertainment that brought great consequences instead of eternal happiness.

A year after being called to the kingdom of God, I finally gave my life to Christ. I chose to become a slave of Christ rather than sin. I remember telling my mother that if someone came to me and asked me to exchange the presence of God for a billion dollars, I couldn't do it. *I don't* want to know what it is like to live without God; I won't be able to live without Him.

I've seen so many people who say they love God yet they give in to drugs, alcohol, cigarettes, or pornography. When I ask them why they do those things if they love God, their answers were the same: "It's okay. God loves me and will forgive me," or "I'll ask for forgiveness later." They abused God's forgiveness. Some would tell others how much they loved God, and it is great to spread the Word of God, but none spoke with his or her heart.

There are two types of abusers of forgiveness: one is the abuser who doesn't have the slightest idea about what the Bible says about forgiveness; the other abuser likes to call himself a Christian. These people actually are familiar with Scripture, and then use it, twist it, and take it out of context to justify their behavior and attempt to deceive us.

I know a man who said it was okay for him to have many wives. I told him that the Lord created man and woman, not man and *women*. The man replied, "Solomon had many wives, so why can't I?" I said that he must not have read the whole Solomon story, because the reason for his downfall and the reason for God's leaving him were because he had many wives. It's important that we read the whole chapter, the whole Bible, instead of picking only those verses that we like. It is true that the Bible tells us to forgive others as the Lord forgave us, but there are requirements for forgiveness.

God forgives us only when we come to Him with a spirit of remorse, change our lives through His Son, ask for forgiveness, live with the Word of God and repent. We are not to cheapen the gift of God's forgiveness by treating it with disrespect. By grace we have been saved; it is not from ourselves. It is the gift of God (Ephesians 2:8). The Lord's purpose is to change men's hearts so that they give up their wicked ways and choose to follow Him. Luke 17:3 tell us to forgive those who sin against us if they repent. God does not do meaningless things that do not serve His ultimate purpose of bringing men into His grace and His presence.

There are times when I do get angry with people who keep repeating their sins. I know that as a Christian I must love and be patient but there are times when I just want to smack their head and hope that they'll finally wake up. When I complained to my mother, she would always say, "our job is to warn them." As *Ezekiel 33:7-9* tells us. And despite many attempts by ungodly people to mislead or pressure us, we need to stand firm. Our heavenly Father does not forgive those that refuse to repeat and continue in their sinful ways. Remember, God loves us unconditionally, but there is conditional forgiveness. Our heavenly Father offered to forgives those who come with remorseful hearts, turn away from sinful ways, and to carry our own cross and follow Him.

Are You Ready?

"*Then the kingdom of heaven shall be likened to ten virgins who took their lamps and went out to meet the bridegroom. Now five of them were wise, and five were foolish. Those who were foolish took their lamps and took no oil with them, but the wise took oil in their vessels with their lamps. But while the bridegroom was delayed, they all slumbered and slept. "And at midnight a cry was heard: 'Behold, the bridegroom is coming; go out to meet him!' Then all those virgins arose and trimmed their lamps. And the foolish said to the wise, 'Give us some of your oil, for our lamps are going out.' But the wise answered, saying, 'No, lest there should not be enough for us and you; but go rather to those who sell, and buy for yourselves.' And while they went to buy, the bridegroom came, and those who were ready went in with him to the wedding; and the door was shut. "Afterward the other virgins came also, saying, 'Lord, Lord, open to us!' But he answered and said, 'Assuredly, I say to you, I do not know you.' "Watch therefore, for you know neither the day nor the hour in which the Son of Man is coming."* - Matthew 25:1-13

The first Bible verses that appeared on my arms were from Matthew 25:1-13. At first, I didn't quite look too deeply into the meaning of the Bible verse. I was only thirteen and knew very little about the Bible and the true meaning of walking with God. I never thought about what it meant to be "ready" before those Bible verses appeared.

My mother watches the news and cries and prays for victims of tragedies almost every night. I've always hated watching the news; I can't deal with the pain of knowing that somewhere out there, a situation is hopeless. And each day, news gets worse and worse.

We are coming close to the end time. You can deny it, but it is right in front of your eyes. And this is just the beginning—what will happen when it gets to the end? What will happen when our world turns completely away from God? Victims of tragedies don't know that they will die when they wake up in the morning. People might die in their sleep or when crossing the street. Life is full of uncertainties. We never know when our time on earth is up until it's over. At eighteen years old, I've never been scared of dying. I know that everyone dies eventually, but I have been scared of whether or not I'll go to heaven and scared of whether I am prepared for the day when Jesus Christ will come back.

The first time I came to know God, I had the hardest time understanding Him and His plans. An evangelist I knew taught me the love of God and His blessings but not how to walk with God or what would happen after I accepted God. For many years after I received the gift that I was given, I asked God and myself how I could better serve Him. How could I prepare others and myself to be ready for Him, anytime He wished to come? I found out after three years that all I needed was a step of faith. Faith is so important. We must be ready to live every day with the Word of God and the guidance of the Holy Spirit. An article by Jason Chatraw said, "While we believers have the Holy Spirit with us at all times leading and guiding, there are moments when we are thrust into situations where we must be ready to impact our world for Christ. We are prompted by the Holy Spirit to encourage, challenge, or share with someone. If we are serious about our faith, we must be ready to respond in obedience to His voice."

In the first two years of my walk with God, I had a hard time understanding Him and His plans. His plans weren't complicated, but I was making them complicated. I wanted to be in control and had a hard time with letting God take control. I didn't learn to have faith in God in just a day; it was a step-by-step process.

Every day we are to practice in the words of God. We must wake up by welcoming the Holy Spirit to guide us and ask for wisdom to be with us throughout the day. We must be ready for Him whenever He decides to come. We must ask ourselves every day if we are ready. No one knows the time or day that He will come. He could come at any time.

A few days after the handwriting appeared, the words "I am coming soon" appeared more than once. My family and I found out that when the letters were important, they came more than once. When we told others that God was making the plans to come soon, they expressed disbelief. I was shocked, because clearly in the Bible, Jesus did say that He was coming back to get His brides. Jesus Christ's coming back shouldn't be news, yet some people had the hardest time believing it.

A pastor once came to our house and told me to stop spreading the word about God's coming soon. He said that so many disciples of God—evangelists and prophets—over the years had said many times that God was coming soon, yet He has not come yet. But have you ever wondered if maybe it's not that He hasn't come but rather that He is waiting? "The Lord is not slow in keeping his promises, as some understand slowness. He is patient with you, not wanting anyone to perish, but everyone to come to repentance" (2 Peter 3:9).

When you look at everything in this world, you can tell that we are no longer waiting for the time but that we are already in the middle of the "time." God can no longer wait for us. The world is drowning in sin. Material things and earthly entertainment blind us. We depend on the government and the president rather than depending on God. We can't be taking all the time in the world. He could come tomorrow, today, or at this very moment. Can you honestly look at your heart and say you put God first in your life and that you are ready?

We must ask ourselves if we are ready every minute and every second of our lives. I encourage you to pray, to reflect, and to examine your heart. Ask yourself: am

I preparing myself, making myself "ready" (Rev. 19:7) to be Christ's bride? Are we Spirit-filled, Word-filled, holy, radiant, and blameless? Are we living a life of righteous acts and is sincerely devoted to Jesus, our heavenly bridegroom? Being the bride of Christ means we stand firm in our faith and wait for Christ's return.

Many Will Seek to Enter Heaven, but Few Will Enter

"At that time Michael, the great prince who protects your people, will arise. There will be a time of distress such as has not happened from the beginning of nations until then. But at that time your people—everyone whose name is found written in the book—will be delivered." —Daniel 12:1

When I was first taken to heaven, I met Abraham in front of the golden entrance. I asked him why there is an entrance in heaven, and Abraham answered, "Not everyone can enter into heaven. Few have tried" At one entrance; there was an angel with a big gold book. People were lining up in front of the angel. Those whose names were not in the book were carried to the pit of fire—that was the closest thing to hell that I've experienced. I found as I grew older that Revelation 20:15 also explained the book of life. Those whose names are in the book have entrance to heaven.

Before I become a Christian, I heard preachers say that if we become Christians, we can go to heaven. I later learned that we couldn't go to heaven simply by being "Christians." When we accept Jesus Christ as our one and only Savior, we must also accept the Holy Spirit to guide us toward leading a Christ-centered life. I also learned that without the Holy Spirit to guide us, we cannot lead a life the way that God wants.

Reading Bible, giving tithes, going to church regularly, and helping others will not lead to an eternal life with God. I'm not saying that these are not good things, but when you are turning into a lifeless person, then you know you're not leading a Christ-centered life. I know some people who go to church regularly, pray, read the Bible, and live a life of stability. Those same people constantly judge others, talk behind other people's back, and need to constantly be in other people's business. One guy said, "You'll know when the rapture come just by looking at me." He's pretty much saying that there won't be the rapture without him. I feel that many of us tend to take advantage of God's love and "assume that we are good soil," as Francis Chan put it in his book *Crazy Love*. We feel that just by looking at someone's outer appearance—money, family, house, or income—we can judge who is going to heaven. We simply cannot build a personal relationship with God and know what He wants when money, addictions, material things, and earthy entertainment take top priority in our minds and hearts.

You might say that you donate regularly to charity, do good things in the name of God, attend church regularly, keep all commandments, and do all things a Christian should, but so did the rich man who was trying to justify himself before Jesus (Matthew 19:16-20).

The one thing many Christians forget is that the most important part of being a Christian is to follow Christ and put Him above everything else—and then everything will fall in to place.

The year I experienced the gate to heaven was the same year—2009—when an uninvited couple came to White House Correspondents Association dinner. I feel that it was no coincidence that it happened, because that was close to how it is in heaven. The couple said that they were invited, but the White House said that they weren't on the guest list. Many Christians right now might be saying, "Oh, I'm going to heaven all right. I have already accepted Jesus Christ as my Savior." But those same Christians might be the people whose names are not in the Book of Life. I am telling you right now that going to church is not the way to heaven. Religion is not the way to heaven. Charity is not the way to heaven. Doing wonderful works is not the way to heaven. Volunteering in every church meeting is not the way to heaven. Baptism is not the way to heaven.

Now don't get me wrong. Going to church regularly, giving to charity, and doing wonderful work are very good things in a Christian life, but so many times, we put all on that list as our top priorities. We forget that above everything else, Jesus is the way to heaven. Leading a Christ-centered life, having faith in God, solely living for God, and putting Him above everything else is the way to heaven. Do not establish your own righteousness; instead, rest in the righteousness of Christ Jesus.

Without God in Heaven

Wherever I go to give testimony, many people are very interested to hear about heaven. They constantly ask me about my experience in heaven, and some ask me to pray to God to let them visit heaven. I don't have the authority or the right to ask God to give them anything. I am only an unworthy sinner who is anointed by God, simply because He loves me. So their request to visit heaven always makes me a bit upset. Their focus seems to be heaven, not God. I recently read *Crazy Love* by Francis Chan, and he quoted John Piper's book, *God is the Gospel*. Piper asked whether we are in love with God:

"The critical question for our generation—and for every generation—is this: If you could have heaven, with no sickness, and with all the friends you ever had on earth, and all the food you ever liked, and all the leisure activities you ever enjoyed, and all the natural beauties you ever saw, all the physical pleasures you ever tasted, and no human conflict or any natural disasters, could you be satisfied with heaven, if Christ were not there?"

This really got me thinking. I am in love with God. Although I have experienced heaven many times, my enjoyment and happiness with heaven isn't because of the greater things in heaven but with the presence of God. If God were not in heaven, then heaven would mean nothing to me. I would like to have a life of stability, where I don't have to worry about money, house or financial problems, racism, or school. But eternal happiness is with God.

I'm sure all the millionaires, billionaires, royals, and celebrities experience the heaven without God. When we look at them, they seem to be the happiest people on earth, with no financial problems, living a stable life. Yet even though these people have all things that I don't have, I think that they are not happy. There never seems to be "enough" for them.

As a girl who isn't leading a stable life in any way and who still continually struggles in every way, I never have worried. There is no deep fear crawling up my heart or heavy burdens on my shoulder. I choose to trust in God and be in His presence. Sometimes I wonder if I have any emotion or if I am even human. This peacefulness and joy that fills my heart in the presence of my heavenly Father is the only emotion I've known since I was fifteen years old, when I finally let God take the control.

People ask me what I think my purpose for God is, and my answer is always the same: it is to serve Him. I am not mine; there is nothing on earth that is mine. I am His. He gives me everything I own. I'm not a robot that is being controlled, nor am I in the hands of an abusive father who scares me. I am in the hands of my loving Father, to whom I choose to give my life. Only with God will we find our eternal happiness.

What I've learned

In 2009 I was a foolish child who had little knowledge of the Bible or how to walk with God. I was tossed left to right by people who felt that they had the right to say what they wanted, because they had more experience. Over the past five years, God has taught me so much. I learned to trust God, to leave my pride, and to let Him take full control. I learned that I am nothing without God. I own nothing. My body, my soul, and my spirit are His. Over these past years, I've gone through more hardships, emotionally and mentally, then I would like to in this life time but I learn that when things don't seem to go your way, be patient. God has a better plan for you. He wants to give you the BEST! When you feel alone, know that you are not. You have a friend in God. He is always right next to you, you just need to open your heart and let Him in. When you feel that you no longer have the strength to go on with life, that's okay. You don't need to do it alone. Lean on God, have faith and let Him take control. The most important weapons you'll need for your walk with God is wisdom, knowledge and understanding.

There were many days when I felt as if I am failing in everything in life, that I disappointed God and that I am not worthy enough to be His daughter. But I know His love, His patience and kindness. I can never turn away from Him. We cannot give up God for earthly entertainment and materialistic things. He has given us His one and only son for our sins. We need to learn to open our eyes and stop feeling sorry for ourselves. We have God by our side and with God, ALL THINGS ARE POSSIBLE.

I pray that as you read this book, you will understand the special gift, writings on the arms, the gift that God had gifted me, and I hope that you fall in love with God all over again. God is unlimited.

Letter to the Reader

I do not know how to convince you about the gift that God gave me. I can only trust the Lord to open your eyes and heart. I do not ask you to praise me or to believe me. I only ask that you have faith in God, believe in Him, and trust in the plans He has for you. I ask that you get ready for the arrival of God every day, as we do not know the time or day when He will come. My job as a disciple of God has always been to tell you that God is coming soon. I wish for you to be ready and to question where you are with your life and the decisions you've made. We live in a world where it is no longer safe anywhere. It is only God to whom we can turn and trust.

"I have fought the good fight, I have finished the race, and I have remained faithful." - 2 Timothy 4:7 (8.21.2008)

Questions with the Author

Why are you writing this book?

- I am writing this book because the Lord told me to write this book. I wanted others to know the true meaning of being a disciple of Jesus Christ. I also wanted to share my experience in Heaven and who God is. I wanted others to know Him as well. I write this book mostly to let others know that there is no limit when it comes to God. I want others to know about His second coming. His message is loud and clear in the writings on my arms. I want others to focus solely on God and His message, not the writing on my flesh.

Why write the book five years after it happened?

- God first told me to write this book in 2009, but because I was only thirteen year old at the time and was criticized, I felt that I was not experienced enough to write a book. I had been running away from my responsibility as the disciple of Jesus Christ for the past five years, simply because I was scared.

I was much like Jonah, who ran away from God simply because he did not like the Assyrians' wicked ways or because he was afraid of going. I too was afraid of the hate and disapprove look of others. At that time, I simply did not have motivation to write a book. I felt that no one would believe the words of a thirteen-year-old, and I wanted to make sure I would not follow the wicked ways. I am eighteen years old now and am much wiser. I trust in the Lord with all my heart, and the Lord has "punished" me enough for not following His plans. I know how to separate words in my head, words from others, and the words of God. My family and I prayed a lot before we wrote this book. We did not want to write this book without making sure that we got His blessing. God always has the perfect timing for His plans, and this is the right time for the book to be written. All praise and glory belong to God.

How old were you when the writing came?

-   When the Lord first anointed me in the summer of 2008, I was thirteen years old. When the writing on my arms first appeared, I was fourteen years old. I was born in August 19,1995. The handwriting had appeared on December 14,2008.

How do you feel when the writing came on your arms? Does it hurt?

-   Many people have asked me this. I do not feel any pain. The gift is from the Lord; He would not bring harm to my body. When the writing came on the arms, all I feel is tingling sensation all over my arms. It does not hurt. Even though there have been a total of 900 writings, there are no scars on my arms. It is the gift of God after all.

Did you do the writing on your arms by yourself?

- In the beginning, there were many people who thought that I did the writings on my arms by myself. Others would say that the writings were from Satan. I was judge rather very harshly. Where would a thirteen-year-old girl get the idea of writing Bible verses on her arms? It is not possible, with human ability, to write 900 Bible verses and phrases without any scars. And IF I did write the writings by myself, I would have stop a long time ago. I wouldn't have had to endure the hardships and trials that came with the writing. I do not want any attention, fame or fortune. If the writing was from Satan, then why were all the writings Bible verses? Why would Satan go out of his way to praise God and ask God children to go back to Him? Why would Satan warn us about Jesus Christ second coming? As I mentioned in this book, I have nothing to gain from inventing this story.

What is it like to be a follower of Jesus Christ at such a young age?

- It's hard, but I wouldn't trade it for anything else in the world. I have very few friends, not because I don't want friends but because it is hard to meet one who is committed to God, someone who accepts the gift that the Lord had given me. As I've mentioned, former friends have abandoned me. Although now I have forgiven them, the feeling of distrust never really goes away. I am now a bit more cautious and socially reserved. When you are gifted differently, many adults around you become more cautious and tend to judge you rather harshly. My family and I have met many difficulties, we still do, but God has won against them all. I feel that once you personally know God, His love, His mercy, His kindness - you would never be able to turn your back on God again. There are many temptations, hardships, and trials but once you have God, all you feel is peace and joy rather then unhappiness and pain. I am still not perfect, I make many mistakes and sometime can't hear the voice of God due to all the distractions in the world but I am learning every day. I know that I am nothing without God.

How do you feel about the gift that God had gifted you?

- Some people might criticize me for the gift that God has given me, but it is what it is. Only God can be the judge. I have nothing to hide or be ashamed of. There were a total of around nine hundred writings that appeared on my arms. Some days there would ten writings that constantly changed. All things are possible with God. I understand that people have a hard time believing the writings, because even I, at one point, had a hard time believing that the writing on my arms was from God. But as years goes by, He remind faithful and patient with me. I know myself the most. I know what my heart is made of. I know how I feel when the anointed fire of the Holy Spirit overcomes my body but above all, I know my heavenly Father.

What is your future plans?

- Is scary for me to say this, but I have none. I go along with the plans that God has for me. I would like to have the experience of a missionary and meet with other disciples of God. I am hoping to go to Christian university once I finish my community college and study medicine or theology. I would like to help others. I know the feeling of having nothing. My family and I plan to help others, especially families and elders. I wish to be a voice for God and to bring the Good News to the world. There are still many things to learn and many improvements to make, but I trust God. I believe that as I grow older, He will teach me many things. But at the end of the day, no matter how many plans I have, it is only God who can decide for me.

How many times did you go to heaven?

- In total, I believe is around 5-7 times. We have lost count after the third time. Each trip to heaven never last longer then an hour.

What is the main message behind this book and the writing on your arms?

- The main message behind the writing is that HE IS COMING! The end times are here. I was thirteen years old when the Lord shared this message but because I was a child who had no courage and no ability, I could not spread the message. I am now eighteen years old and according to United States, an adult, I feel that it is time for me to stand up for my faith and spread the good news of Lord!

How should one prepare for the Lord coming?

The first thing Jesus tells us to do is keep alert: Jesus is coming again. *Luke 12:35-40* tell us to be dressed in readiness. The Lord will come in two stages: the first stage is called "the day of Christ" (*Philippians 1:10*) and the second stage is called "the day of the Lord", which occur at the end of seven-year tribulation. We are to be ready at every second and every minute of every day for we do not know when the Lord will come.

- The second thing is to remain faithful. This is what Jesus said, "Peter asked, "Lord, is that illustration just for us or for everyone?" And the Lord replied, "A faithful, sensible servant is one to whom the master can give the responsibility of managing his other household servants and feeding them. If the master returns and finds that the servant has done a good job, there will be a reward. I tell you the truth, the master will put that servant in charge of all he owns. But what if the servant thinks, 'My master won't be back for a while,' and he begins beating the other servants, partying, and getting drunk? The master will return unannounced and unexpected, and he will cut the servant in pieces and banish him with the unfaithful. "And a servant who knows what the master wants, but isn't prepared and doesn't carry out those instructions, will be severely punished. But someone who does not know, and then does something wrong, will be punished only lightly. When someone has been given much, much will be required in return; and when someone has been entrusted with much, even more will be required."

Why does God only write Bible verses on your arms?

- In the beginning, the writing did not start with Bible verse. People had a hard time accepting the letters, mainly because they believe that if it was not in the Bible then it was not from God. When God did finally decided to write Bible verses, people had an ever-harder time believing in the writing was from God because there has never been a gift such as mine in the Bible. But you must realize that it is supernatural, one of the spiritual gift.

What do these Bible verses mean?

- To me, every word, every verse in the Bible is very important. God had written these verses on my arms to point out answers for us when we are stuck in a situation that we have no answer to. One must pray, open our heart to the Lord and ask the Holy Spirit to teach the word to us before we can really understand the meaning of the verse.

The handwritings:

- After much analyzing, we find that there are three different people writing these writings. The reason we think that is because the handwritings are quite different. Some would look beautiful while others would look as if they were written in a rush. We can't quite explain it but if you look at all the pictures, you can see the different handwritings.

Are you Baptized?

- This might seem like an odd question but many have asked me this before. This became controversial subject around 2010-2012, mainly in my church. I was baptized three times. The first time was when I was a baby, as my father's side of the family is Catholic. I was christened as a baby. The second time, I was baptized in heaven. The river I was christened was flowing with gold. The third time, a close pastor friend of our family baptized me at my aunt house.

What I wish for the readers?

- I wish that you would read this book with an open mind. I hope that this book would only strengthen your faith and relationship with God, not weaken it. I wish that you would look past the gift and focus solely on the message behind the writings on my arms. I pray that this book would bring many blessings to your life and to those around you.

Notes:

- In the book, I did not write anyone names because I did not want to point finger at anyone. The book is mainly to focus on God, the message behind the gift and my journey to finding the real meaning of being disciple of Jesus Christ.
- The "questions with author" were questions that many had asked over the past five years. If you do have any other questions or wish to talk to me, please email <u>Sophia.arabella77@gmail.com</u>.

Sources:

Andrew Wommack. "Don't Limit God"

Francis Chan. (2008). Crazy love. David C Cook.

Jason Chatraw. Being the Bride of Jesus Christ: How you can relate. Lifeway.

The Way finding Bible, New Living Translation. Tyndale House Publishing, Inc.

Bible Gateway, a division of The Zondervan Corporation. Internet.

Printed in the United States
By Bookmasters